MW00658044

THE TOMÁS CRUZ CONGA METHOD

VOLUME I • BEGINNING
Conga Technique As Taught In Cuba

by **Tomás Cruz**
with Kevin Moore,
Mike Gerald and Orlando Fiol

Online Video

Video
dv.melbay.com/20299

You Tube
www.melbay.com/20299V

Cover Design: Bill Wolfer bill@mamborama.com
Recording studio photos: Tom Ehrlich tjejazz@sbcglobal.net
DVD Recorded at: Little Gypsy Studios, Santa Cruz, CA
Skin on Skin Congas provided by: Javier Muñiz

1 2 3 4 5 6 7 8 9 0

Visit us on the Web at www.melbay.com — E-mail us at email@melbay.com

Table of Contents

Group 2: Exercises for the Tip Stroke and Manoteo

PART 5: RUDIMENTS AND SOLOING

PART 6: MARCHA EXERCISES

PART 7: MARCHAS

PART 8: RECURSOS

APPENDIX 1: CLAVE

APPENDIX 2: MARCHAS WRITTEN IN 8TH NOTES

APPENDIX 3: TOMÁS CRUZ – SELECTED DISCOGRAPHY

ADDITIONAL PHOTOS

Preface to the Tomás Cruz Conga Method Book/GYG Series

The Mystery of Modern Cuban Conga Playing

Most congueros, whether students or professionals, quickly find themselves on an emotional roller coaster when they first go to Cuba or to hear a modern Cuban band on tour. It begins with shock – the level of musicianship, even among 12 and 13 year old kids, is astounding. Shock gives way to euphoria as the newcomer realizes that he or she has just stumbled on perhaps the most creative chapter in the history of Latin music. Euphoria gives way to a determination to learn this new style, and finally, confusion and frustration reign supreme! Latin percussion usually involves learning a different set of fairly strict rhythmic patterns for each style, but what patterns are these Cubans using? The groove is overwhelming, but the conguero almost seems to be improvising. It's hard to pick out the pattern because it keeps changing, and the same problems come up when trying to analyze the patterns of the drums, timbales, bongó, bass and piano.

The next step, of course, is to seek help, but the vast majority of teachers and methods, both inside and outside of Cuba, begin by teaching basic historical rhythms and never seem to get to what's actually being played in today's Cuban concerts. And most videos and method books by famous virtuoso congueros tend to focus on soloing or pedagogic exercises rather than the actual content of the recordings and concerts which inspired the student's interest in the first place. The magical groove of the modern Cuban rhythm section remains a mystery.

Solving the Mystery – The Story of the Tomás Cruz Conga Method

We were determined not to let these books fall into the same traps as their predecessors, so to ensure we'd get to the final goal, we started at the end and worked backwards. We tackled Volume III first, immersing ourselves in the real music that's being played in the nightclubs and concert halls of Havana today – the music of the leading bands of Cuba – Paulito FG, Manolín (El Médico de la Salsa), Los Van Van, NG La Banda, Bamboleo, Klimax, Issac Delgado, Manolito y su Trabuco, Charanga Habanera, Carlos Manuel, Azúcar Negra, etc. As anyone who's heard these bands live will testify, you can study Mambo, Guaracha and Salsa for a lifetime and still have no idea whatsoever what the congueros are doing in this type of music!

So our first step was to find one of the leading congueros of the modern Cuban style and we were lucky enough to discover that our dream candidate had recently moved to Miami and was willing to take on the project. Tomás "Tomasito" Cruz grew up in the middle of the musical revolution that took place in Havana in the 90's. It was he who invented and performed the ground-breaking conga parts on perhaps the greatest Timba album ever recorded, Paulito FG's "Con la conciencia tranquila". After relocating to Miami in 1998, he joined another of the leading Timba bands, "Manolín, El Médico de la Salsa". He also plays with top traditional Latin artists such as Celia Cruz and Willie Chirino.

The second step was to cut through the verbiage and ask Tomás to demonstrate *exactly* what he plays, all the way through, on specific songs from Paulito FG's legendary "Con la conciencia tranquila" and various Timba classics from Tomasito's current group, "El Médico de la Salsa". We videotaped him playing along with his own recordings and then asked him to study the video footage, explain his approach, analyze the arrangement as a whole, and isolate key patterns and techniques. For each rhythm taught in Volume III, we tell you exactly where to find it on a specific recording. These are not "etudes" or exercises invented for the sake of writing a method book – this is the real deal.

The next task was to present the rhythms in such a simple way that readers would be able to learn them quickly and without frustration – not just watch the DVD once and then file it away with the other method books for future reference. We created a simple and clear notation system which combines standard rhythmic notation with easy to understand letters which can be easily read those who don't read music, and then we went a step further by inventing the **Step by Step DVD Method**, which makes it fast and easy to learn the patterns without even looking at the book. An equally important advantage of the DVD method is that, instead of spending time trying to decipher printed notation, all of the student's practice time is spent in rhythm, watching one of the world's funkiest congueros and absorbing the intangible nuances of his technique and body language.

Satisfied that Volume III had accomplished its goal, we began Volume II, which covers the roots of Timba – the Cuban, Afro-Cuban and non-Cuban rhythms invented prior to 1990 which formed the rhythmic vocabulary of the Timba pioneers – rhythms such as Songo, Mozambique, Bomba, Guaguancó, 6/8, etc. Volume II also uses the Step by Step DVD Method, but the rhythms are considerably easier. Like Volume III, Volume II gives you the music history to go with the patterns and identifies classic recordings on which they can be found.

Finally, we wrote Volume I, in which Tomasito reveals the time-tested conga method which he himself studied with Changuito and other master congueros at the ENA conservatory in Havana. Volume I starts at the absolute beginning and is designed for the person who has never touched the congas, but is also of great value to the advanced player who wishes to understand the foundation and rudiments of the approach that has allowed the ENA and the other Havana conservatories to consistently turn out so many world-class congueros each year. Volume I begins with simple exercises to develop technique and systematically works its way to basic rhythm patterns such as Salsa, Chachachá and Bolero, which are presented using the Step by Step DVD method. It also contains an extensive series of rudiments and "recursos" for use in solos and fills. This is continued in Volume II.

The Tomás Cruz Conga Method
Volume II - Intermediate
Essential Cuban Conga Rhythms
Mel Bay Catalog #20300DP

The Tomás Cruz Conga Method
Volume III - Advanced
Timba: Modern Cuban Conga Rhythms
Mel Bay Catalog #20301DP

ACKNOWLEDGEMENTS

Tomás Cruz: Este libro es el resultado de mucho estudio, sacrificio y dedicación, el mismo no se pudiera haber escrito sin la ayuda de muchas personas, a las cuales quiero darles mi agradecimiento.

Tuve mis primeros estudios en la E.V.A. (Escuela Vocacional de Arte) en Pinar del Río, Cuba, donde mis maestros fueron muy estrictos y grandiosos (Gilberto, Tomas Torre, Néstor Luis y Héctor). También quiero agradecer a mis maestros de solfeo, historia de la música, piano, etc.

A mis grandes amigos y compañeros de estudios de mi año (Omar Rojas, Ciro Parlá, Eddie Pérez, Jorge Castillo, Iván González, Iliana Castillo, Ademilis Hernández) que fueron consejeros y compañía en mi vida.

Vale reconocer la presencia de una persona, a la cual yo quiero y admiro mucho: José Luis Quintana (Changuito) por haberme enseñado la belleza, la técnica y la magia de la Conga. Junto a mí, otros estudiantes como Yoel del Sol, Carlos Reyes, Pedro Pablo Martínez, que tuvieron la suerte de haber aprendido este estilo maravilloso.

También quiero mencionar a una persona muy especial en mi vida (Adolfo Orta, mi maestro de trombón, que mas bien no fue maestro, fue un amigo).

Quiero darle las gracias a mi maestro de Batá, Nardo (el Gollo) que me dió la posibilidad de aprender un instrumento tan lindo y rico en ritmo, el cual me ayudó y me dio capacidad en mi mente para mezclar y combinar ritmo de Batá con la Conga.

Es muy importante señalar mis compañeros de banda, Yoel Páez, Yoel Domínguez, Sergio Noroña, Fran Rubio, Yosvel Bernal, Alexander Abreu, Joaquín Díaz, Carlos Pérez, Juan Manuel Ceruto, por haberme ayudado a enriquecer mi mente de su sabiduría.

Quiero hablar sobre la persona más importante en el proceso de este libro, una persona de una inteligencia genial, a la cual le doy las gracias por ser el creador de la idea para hacer este libro: Kevin Moore. Además, agradecer a Mike Gerald por haber dedicado parte de su tiempo para escribir muy rápidamente este método de percusión, y gracias a Orlando Fiol por habernos aconsejado y ayudado con su gran experiencia en la cración de este libro.

Me gustaría mencionar en este agradecimiento los congueros, que fueron mis patrones a seguir: Jorge Alfonso (El Niño) y Angá (Irakere), Andrés Miranda (Negrón), Tomás Ramos, Juan Nogueras (Wickly), Tata Güines, los Papines, el Goyo (maestro del I.S.A.), José Luis Quintana (Changuito), Manolo (Van Van), Yulo (N.G. La Banda), Yoel Drigs, etc.

También quiero darle las gracias a timba.com, Duniel Deya, y a mi gente de California que me ayudaron en mi estancia allá: Michel, Johann, Alexis, Alain, Fito, Bárbara, Javier, Osvaldo, y Joanna.

Espero que este diferente y nuevo método ayude a todos los congueros a desarrollar la técnica de Timba de una manera rápida y eficaz para que el mundo cuente con buenos congueros.

English translation by Tanja Cruz: This book is the result of many years of studies, sacrifice and dedication and could not have been written without the support of many individuals, whom I would like to acknowledge.

My first studies took place at the E.V.A. Vocational School of Arts (Escuela Vocacional de Arte) in Pinar del Río, Cuba, where I had very strict and magnificent teachers (Gilberto, Tomás Torre, Néstor Luis and Héctor). Among others, I would like to thank my professors of solfeggio, music history and piano.

To my great friends and fellow students of my graduating class (Omar Rojas, Ciro Parlá, Eddie Pérez, Jorge Castillo, Iván González, Iliana Castillo, Ademilis Hernández) who gave me advice and were companions in my life.

I'd also like to acknowledge the presence of a person whom I greatly respect and admire: José Luis Quintana (Changuito) for teaching me the beauty, technique and magic of the Conga. Along with me, other students like Yoel del Sol, Carlos Reyes, Pedro Pablo Martínez had the opportunity to learn this marvelous style.

I would like to mention another special person in my life, Adolfo Orta, my trombone teacher, who was not just my teacher but my friend as well.

I want to express my gratitude to my teacher of Batá, Nardo (el Goyo) who gave me the opportunity to learn an instrument so beautiful and rich in rhythm, who helped me and allowed me to combine the rhythms of Batá with the Conga.

It's very important acknowledge the musicians with whom I played and recorded: Yoel Páez, Yoel Domínguez, Sergio Noroña, Frank Rubio, Yosvel Bernal, Alexander Abreu, Joaquín Díaz, Carlos Pérez, Juan Manuel Ceruto, for helping me enrich my mind with their knowledge.

I would like to talk about the most important person in the process of creating this book, a person of great intelligence, whom I thank for creating the idea to make this book: Kevin Moore. Also, to thank Mike Gerald for having dedicated some of his time to write with great speed this method of percussion and Orlando Fiol for having given us the benefit of his great experience in the creation of these books.

In this acknowledgment, I'd also like to mention the conga players who were my models to follow: Jorge Alfonso (El Niño) and Angá (Irakere), Andrés Miranda (Negrón), Tomás Ramos, Juan Nogueras (Wickly), Tata Güines, los Papines, el Goyo (teacher at I.S.A.), José Luis Quintana (Changuito), Manolo (Los Van Van), El Yulo (NG La Banda), Yoel Drigs, etc.

I would also like to express my gratitude to timba.com, Duniel Deya, and to my friends in California who helped me during my stay over there: Michel, Johann, Alexey Berlind, Alain, Fito, Bárbara Valladares, Javier, Osvaldo, and Joanna Goldberg.

I hope that this new and different method will help all conga players develop their Timba technique in a fast and efficient way, so that the world will soon see more good conga players.

Kevin Moore, Mike Gerald & Orlando Fiol wish to thank:

Conceptual Guidance: David Peñalosa, Alexey Berlind, and Pepe Martínez.
Production: Neal Hellman, Sarah Belden, Jon Hansen, Doug Witherspoon, Ed Riegler, Christy Meyer, Bill Bay, Trevor Salloum, and above all, our graphics gurus, Bill Wolfer and "Mig".
Photography: Tom Ehrlich (additional photos by Kevin Moore, Duniel Deya and Yoel Páez)
Moral and Technical Support: Wendy Black, Kathryn Van Eenoo, Tanja Cruz, Jorge Ginorio, Juan Tomás García, Javier Muñiz, Mike Lazarus, José Reyes, Mike Doran, María Carlota Domandi, Luis Carranza, Joanna Goldberg, Elena Peña & Nikki, Bruce Ishikawa, Majela Serrano, Hugo Cancio, Arnaldo Vargas, Nina "La Reina del Merengue" Gómez, Mike Croy, and Curtis Lanoue.
Inspiration: Rebeca Mauleón-Santana, Alberto Centelles, Juan Ceruto, Edduar Bernal, Yosvel Bernal, Yoel Páez, Yoel Domínguez, Giraldo Piloto, Calixto Oviedo, Reinier Guerra, Yulién Oviedo, Sonny Bravo, Marty Sheller, Andrés Cuayo, Sergio Noroña, Carlos Caro, and above all, Tomás Cruz for his patience, perseverance and incredible insights into the secrets of music.

All recording session photography by Tom Ehrlich.

10

PART 1: INTRODUCTION

Introduction to the Series: The Tomás Cruz Conga Method

What?

The Tomás Cruz Conga Method is designed to quickly and comprehensively teach anyone, from a rank beginner to a professional conguero, to play congas as they're played in Cuba today. It can be studied using only the books, only the DVD's (Digital Video Disc), or a combination of the two.

Who?

Tomás "Tomasito" Cruz was born and raised in Cuba in the middle of the musical revolution of the 90's. By the time he relocated to Miami he had become one of the top congueros in Cuba, playing in what most Cuban music experts consider one of the two or three best Timba bands ever assembled, the 1997-98 incarnation of Paulito FG y su Élite which recorded the groundbreaking CD, "Con la conciencia tranquila". The creativity and drive of Tomasito's conga tumbaos on that album put him in the very upper echelon of the most competitive Latin music scene in the world. Similarly, it took Tomasito very little time to rise to the top of the Miami Latin music scene, playing with Manolín, el Médico de la Salsa, Willie Chirino, Celia Cruz, and many others. He also has a thorough mastery of bongó, Batá, and a deep understanding of Cuban music as a whole. In short, when we set out to write a book explaining the mysteries of Cuban conga playing, Tomasito was our first choice by a considerable margin.

Why?

For many years it was extremely difficult to find recordings of modern Cuban music, much less to hear the bands live, but in the late 90's groups like Los Van Van and Paulito FG y su Élite began to tour the US, Europe and Japan, and Latin music fans and musicians alike were amazed when they heard the exciting new "Timba" style they were playing. Every instrument of the rhythm section had taken a quantum leap in terms of complexity and creative freedom. However, many of those who tried to learn this new approach found it significantly more difficult to understand than the Salsa commonly played outside of Cuba.

Problem #1: What exactly are they playing? Even those who have taken study courses in Cuba, which invariably seem limited to the fundamentals and history of traditional Cuban music, have found themselves just as dumbfounded upon hearing the modern groups in performance. In addition to the language and cultural barriers, the music is too new for the players themselves to have fully analyzed it...they're too busy *playing* it and adding to it to take time to dissect it and explain it. The albums themselves have so much going on that even professional musicians have difficulty transcribing individual parts by ear and the Timba style is so ambi-dextrous that even knowing whether to slap with the left or right hand becomes part of the jigsaw puzzle.

Solution: All of the patterns in Volume III are from real Timba albums, clearly notated, and spoon-fed to the reader stroke by stroke by means of a simple DVD method.

Problem #2: Where did all of these new ideas come from? The musicians cite the influences of Songo, Batá music, Rumba, Guaguancó, and even American funk and R&B, but what are these rhythms and how are they incorporated into Timba?

Solution: Volume II uses the same innovative teaching techniques to teach the rhythms and offers insights and listening recommendations to help the student grasp their significance.

Problem #3: How do they make it look so easy? These young musicians play with such fire and grace that trying to emulate them can be discouraging. How, without having been born and raised in Havana, can musicians get a little piece of that magic into their own playing?

Solution: Volume I spells out the method used to teach congas in the Cuban conservatories and the hours of DVD footage included in this course provide the opportunity to learn the feel of Cuban drumming by osmosis; to watch and play along with a master conguero as he breaks each pattern down note by note, with a steady rhythm groove playing throughout the exercise.

How?

At the heart of the Tomás Cruz Conga Method is a simple and effective DVD technique based on learning by imitation. Once you understand the simple process explained below, it's actually quite possible to learn each pattern with only the DVD, without reading music at all.

Tomasito plays the pattern at full speed, and then, in slow motion, accompanied by a special click track, he plays only the first stroke of the pattern and then waits for the beginning of the pattern to come around again. He repeats just the first stroke a total of 4 times. This gives the student 4 chances to learn and practice the hand movement, allowing Tomasito's tone, posture, time feel and technique to be assimilated "by osmosis", as he himself assimilated it by watching the greatest congueros of earlier generations during his childhood and adolescence in Cuba.

Tomás then adds the second stroke and repeats *this* cycle 4 times; then the third, and so on until the pattern is complete. It's extremely easy to keep up with the flow of the DVD because only a single stroke is added every four repetitions, and since each DVD chapter can be started over without the tedious rewinding necessary with a video tape, it's easy to go back to the beginning if you lose your place in the pattern. Thanks to the huge capacity of DVD discs, we were able to film Tomasito patiently building many of the patterns in this way. From the very beginning the student is playing in rhythm, and in clave, asked to learn only a single stroke at a time, and given the chance to master it before each additional stroke is added. Patterns that are too long to be appropriate for this method are demonstrated at full speed and in slow motion.

About the Coauthors

Kevin Moore is the music editor of the world's largest Cuban music website, www.timba.com, and the musical director of the American salsa band Orquesta Gitano (www.picadillo.com/gitano). He has studied with dozens of leading Cuban musicians, written many extensive articles on Cuban music, and served as a consultant for features and articles produced by the BBC, the Los Angeles Times, and musicologists from Harvard and other major universities.

Michael Gerald is a Canadian drummer who has spent 7 years studying and playing Timba and has recorded two albums with his group, Sol y Soul (solysoul.timba.com), which, aside from himself, is composed entirely of all-stars from the various Cuban supergroups.

Orlando Fiol, a professional pianist/conguero/composer in the Philadelphia area, began his studies of Latin music as a small child under the tutelage of his father, Latin recording artist Henry Fiol. In 1996 he traveled to Cuba where he studied and played with Pancho Quinto, Changuito, members of Sierra Maestra, Raíces Profundas and the Sexteto Habanero. He is also an expert in the fields of Jazz, classical music and Indian music, having been awarded a fellowship to study tabla and pakhawaj in India. Orlando's encyclopedic knowledge of the history of folkloric and Latin music, and his ability to communicate with Tomasito in fluent Spanish have proved indispensable in the writing of this series.

What is Timba?

Timba is the commonly accepted term for the new type of concert and dance music that's been played in Cuba since about 1989. While he plays all forms of Latin and Afro-Cuban folkloric music, Tomás Cruz is best know for his work with Timba groups, and it was this work that inspired the creation of this series.

Until the late 90's, it was impossible to hear live Timba without going to Cuba, and nearly as hard to acquire Timba recordings. To further complicate matters, music produced in Cuba was and still is, to a great degree, "blacklisted" in the United States and nearly never played on commercial radio. In spite of all these obstacles, Timba groups have been touring the United States and Europe regularly for the last 6 years and have inspired a rapidly growing, almost fanatic following, including American musicians such as coauthors Kevin Moore, Michael Gerald and Orlando Fiol.

The musical genre most closely related to Timba is Salsa, but Timba also contains strong influences from Afro-Cuban folkloric music, American R&B, Jazz, and various other forms of world pop music. A huge emphasis is placed on originality — not only in songwriting and arranging, but in the individual patterns played by each member of the rhythm section, and while this has resulted in a large number of classic recordings, it's also led to a great deal of frustration among musicians trying to learn to play Timba because the rhythm patterns are sometimes unique to each song. Helping people understand this wide range of rhythmic diversity is the primary goal of this series of books.

To learn more about Timba we recommend the website www.timba.com, which contains well over 100,000 words of articles and interviews edited by coauthor Kevin Moore (kevin@timba.com). There are also extensive audio examples and educational materials.

Who are the Leading Timba Bands?

There are about a dozen major Timba groups, with new ones springing up from time to time, and frequent shifting of key players from one band to another. The musical scene in Havana is so strong and closely-knit that each band seems to feed off the creativity of the others.

The most important groups, in approximate order of their appearance on the Timba scene, are Los Van Van, NG La Banda, Charanga Habanera, Issac Delgado, Paulito FG, El Médico de la Salsa, Klimax, Bamboleo, Manolito y su Trabuco, Azúcar Negra, and Los Que Son Son.

Tomás Cruz played with Paulito FG and currently plays with El Médico de la Salsa (also known as Manolín). He played congas on four of the most important albums of the Timba genre:

Paulito FG: "Con la conciencia tranquila" (Nueva Fania NF-108)
Juan Ceruto: "Gracias Formell" (Ciocan Records HMC-2607)
Paulito FG: "El bueno soy yo" (also released as "Paulito FG") (Nueva Fania NF-104)
Manolín, El Médico de la Salsa: "El puente" (Ciocan Records HMC-2605)

Who are the other leading Timba congueros?

There are literally hundreds of phenomenal congueros in Cuba. Here's an incomplete list of some of the leading Timba congueros who tour outside of Cuba frequently. Each has his own page on www.timba.com, as does Tomasito (http://tomasito.timba.com).

Denis "Papacho" Savón
Issac Delgado Group
http://papacho.timba.com

Jorge Luis "Papiosco" Torres
founding member of Klimax
now tours with Cubanismo
http://papiosco.timba.com

Tomás "El Panga" Ramos
Tomasito's predecessor in
Paulito FG y su Élite
http://panga.timba.com

Duñesky Barreto
Bamboleo
http://dunesky.timba.com

Alexis "Mipa" Cuesta
Tomasito's predecessor with
El Médico de la Salsa
http://mipa.timba.com

Orlando Mengual
Charanga Habanera
http://orlandito.timba.com

Jorge "El Toro" Castillo
Los Que Son Son
http://eltoro.timba.com

Evelio Ramos
Manolito y su Trabuco
http://evelio.timba.com

Manuel "Manolo" Labarrera
Los Van Van
http://manolo.timba.com

Luis Guillermo Palacio
Carlos Manuel y su Clan; Sol y Soul

Yoel Cuesta
Azúcar Negra
(now with Adalberto Alvarez)
http://yoelcuesta.timba.com

Adel González
Irakere

Wickly Nogueras
original conguero of NG La Banda
http://wickly.timba.com

Tomás with Duñesky Barreto of Bamboleo
photos by Duniel Deya

PART 2: BASIC HAND POSITION AND POSTURE

Exercise to Develop Proper Posture

Sitting up straight, place the hands flat on the conga so that they form a heart shape.

Next, pull the hands back in a straight line until the phalange (back of the knuckles) reaches the edge of drumhead. In the picture below, Tomasito is pointing to the phalange.

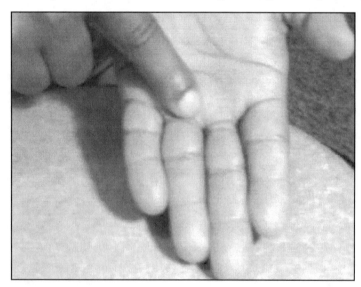

Final position of hands

Side view of correct posture

The idea of the exercise is to be able to cover the entire surface of the drum while minimizing the amount of unnecessary movement of the upper body.

Position of the Legs and Feet

In order to project the sound, the bottom of the conga needs to be tilted off of the ground.

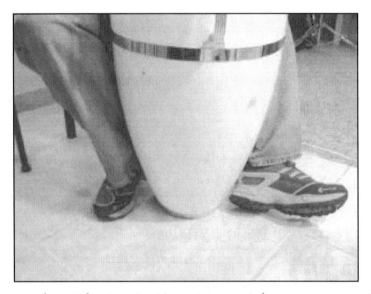

If you're right-handed, the left heel and calf wrap around the conga to comfortably hold it in position while the right foot is placed behind the conga at a 90 degree angle.

PART 3: THE FIVE BASIC STROKES

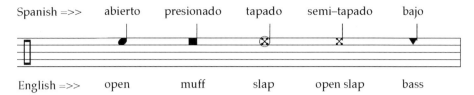

| Spanish =>> | abierto | presionado | tapado | semi–tapado | bajo |
| English =>> | open | muff | slap | open slap | bass |

All conga strokes are produced by some combination of the fingers, the flat of the hand, the palm, and the wrist. Arm weight is used only to add volume. The hand rebounds from the drumskin in the Open and Open Slap strokes, resulting in a ringing tone. The other 3 basic strokes are "closed" or "dry", meaning that the hand and fingers come to rest on the drumskin after striking it. Each basic stroke is thoroughly covered in the exercises and DVD Chapters of Part 4. Secondary strokes such as Tip, Ghost, and Bass-Ghost will be described as they're introduced in the exercises.

OPEN (abierto) – DVD Chapter 1

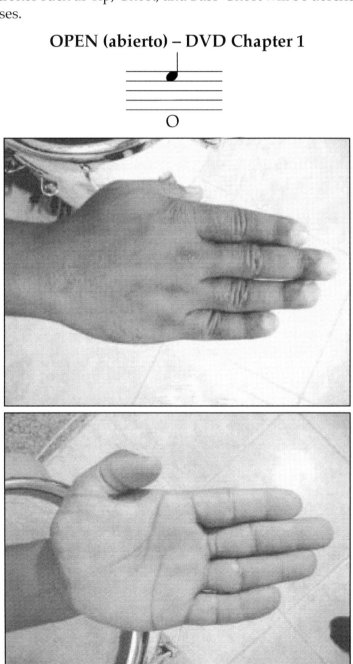

The hand is held so that the fingers and thumb are held tightly together:

19

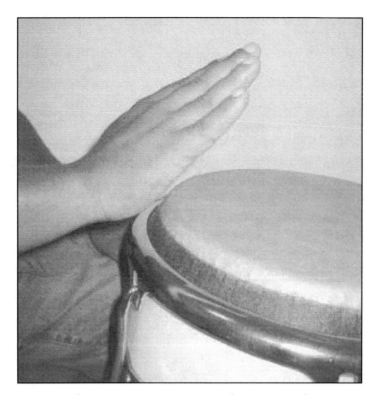

Most of the movement is initiated by the wrist, not the arms.

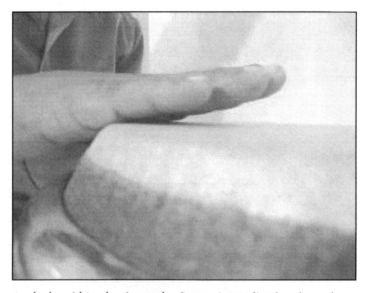

As the hand hits the drum, the fingers immediately rebound upwards, allowing the whole skin to sound.

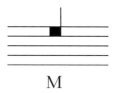

M

We notate the different strokes with different noteheads, such as the square notehead above used to designate the Muff stroke. To make reading even easier, we also add a letter beneath the staff. In the exercises, we add a second line of letters to indicate whether to use the left or right hand.

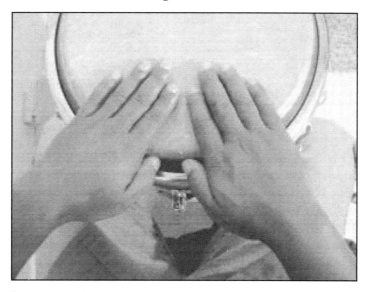

The position of the hands for the Muff stroke is identical to that of the open, but whereas the fingers rebound from the skin for the Open stroke, they remain on the skin at the point of impact for the Muff stroke. As indicated by the Spanish term, *presionado,* a slight pressure is used at the end of the stroke to make it sound dryer and fuller.

INTRODUCTION TO SLAP STROKES

In contrast to the Open and Muff strokes, "slap " strokes use wrist motion and curvature of the fingers to create a vertical whipping action. The hand is closed in the shape of a semicircle and the cupped palm forms a resonant space to amplify the sound. The player should feel vibration in the fingertips after this stroke. In the case of the Open Slap, the fingers rebound immediately after striking the skin to create an open tone which emphasizes the conga's upper harmonics. The closed slap employs the same wrist motion, but rather than rebounding, the fingers are left where they land on the conga head. So, like the Open and Muff strokes, the Open and Closed Slap strokes use the same basic motion and only differ in that in the Open version the fingers rebound to let the tone of the conga ring out.

A variation of the Closed Slap, sometimes called the "pressed slap", involves using the opposite hand to dampen the rest of the conga's surface, creating the ubiquitous popping sound found in most Cuban and Puerto Rican dance music. The opposite hand can be placed in the center of the conga or towards the edge to control the dryness of the sound.

Traditionally, the slap has been predominantly played by the right hand, but modern styles such as Songo and Timba incorporate left hand slaps and the *"doble tapado"* figure which consists of two slaps in succession played by alternate hands. Thus, the exercises in the following section are designed to develop crispness, dynamics and power in both hands when playing slaps.

CLOSED SLAP (tapado) – DVD Chapter 3

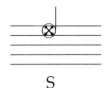

S

The Closed Slap is notated with a circled "X" notehead and an "S" beneath.

The weight of the slap is concentrated on the fingertips, and the movement again comes primarily from the wrist.

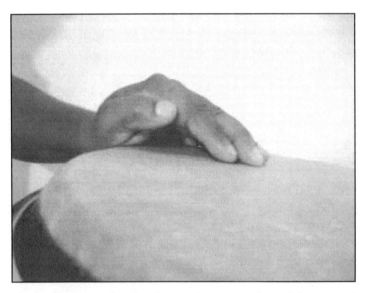

The hand is closed in the shape of a semicircle and the cupped palm forms a resonant space to amplify the sound.

OPEN SLAP (semi-tapado) – DVD Chapter 4

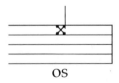

os

The Open Slap is notated with an uncircled "X" notehead and "os" beneath.

The Open Slap uses the same hand position and movement as the Closed Slap, but like the Open stroke, the fingers rebound from the drumhead immediately after the initial impact. Open Slaps are used primarily in soloing.

after impact

BASS (bajo) – DVD Chapter 5

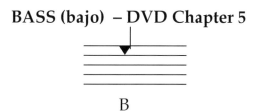

B

The Bass stroke is notated by a downward–pointing triangle

For the Bass stroke, place the fingers slightly apart, with the thumb tightly closed against the hand. The hand comes down flat in the center of the conga. Although often called the "palm" stroke outside of Cuba, it's very important that the whole hand is used and not just the palm.

Sonically speaking, the palm produces a low thud, while the rest of the hand makes the sound sparkle with higher frequency padding that helps it cut through dense musical and rhythmic textures.

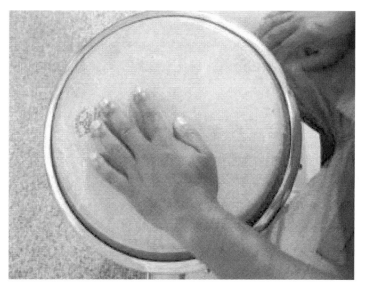

Although often called the "palm" stroke outside of Cuba, it's very important that the whole hand is used and not just the palm.

23

PART 4: EXERCISES

The Havana conservatories have produced a staggering number of brilliant congueros in recent years, many of whose basic training included studying the rigorous and thorough set of exercises presented in Part 4.

For every famous Cuban conguero that has played and recorded outside of the island, there are hundreds more, many of them teenagers, who play at a world-class level. We highly recommend that conga students visit Havana (and also Matanzas and Santiago) to experience the incredible level of musicianship first hand. Those who live in the United States can travel to Cuba legally through programs offered by a variety of companies which specialize in arranging study trips. Students of music, and dance can often arrange to study at one of the Havana conservatories for two weeks. The traveler is very likely to find the vast community of Cuban congueros to be very friendly and eager to share their musical skills and cultural heritage.

Part 4 consists of 36 exercises which have become the standard training method for nearly all conservatory trained modern Cuban congueros. Inspired by the teachings of José Luis "Changuito" Quintana, they cover all the basic and secondary strokes in a comprehensive set of variations, including alternating hands playing the same sounds, the same hands playing different sounds, alternating hands playing different sounds, same hands shifting positions, and opposite hands covering different positions. These exercises also provide a useful introduction to the execution of duple and triple meters, using hand-to-hand or double strokes for duple, but also using hand-to-hand and combinations of single and double strokes to phrase triplets.

In each DVD chapter Tomasito plays the exercise slowly at first, and then gradually increases the speed. Practice along with the DVD and try to emulate Tomasito's posture and technique.

✳✳✳

Group 1: Exercises To Develop the 5 Basic Strokes

The first 30 exercises allow you to systematically master the five basic strokes – first by isolating them and then combining them in various combinations.

The first 3 exercises introduce the Open stroke. The hand is held so that the fingers and thumb are held tightly together. Most of the movement is initiated by the wrist, not the arms. As the hand hits the drum, the fingers immediately angle up, allowing the whole skin to sound.

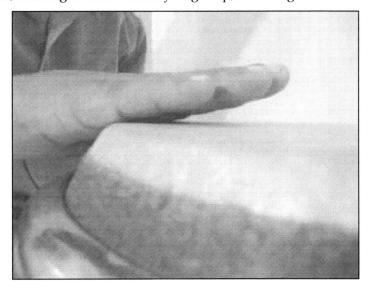

Exercise 1 – DVD Chapter 6

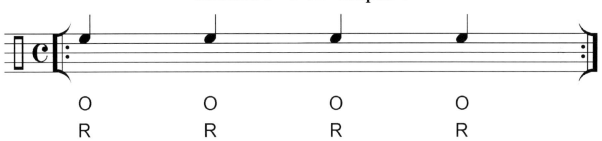

[Througout this series of books, the top row of letters designates the type of stroke ("**O**pen"), and the bottom row indicates which hand is to be used ("**R**ight"). The shape of the notehead also indicates the type of stroke.]

Exercise 2 – DVD Chapter 7

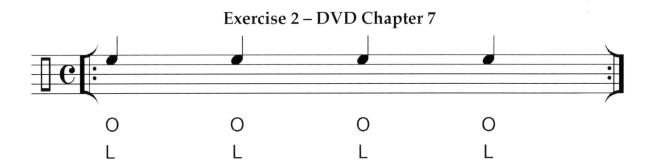

Exercise 3 – DVD Chapter 8

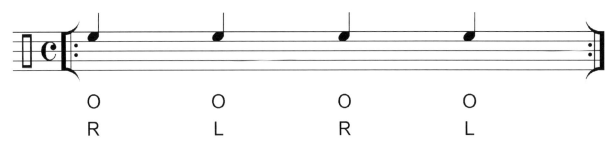

Exercises 4 through 6 introduce another basic stroke, the Closed Slap. The hand is closed in the shape of a semi-circle and the cupped palm forms a resonant space to amplify the sound. The weight of the slap is concentrated on the fingertips, and the movement again comes primarily from the wrist.

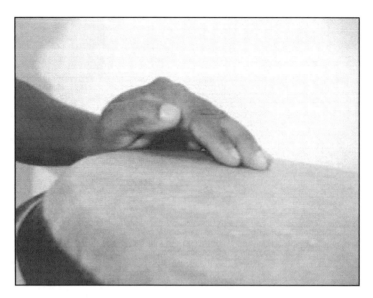

Exercise 4 – DVD Chapter 9

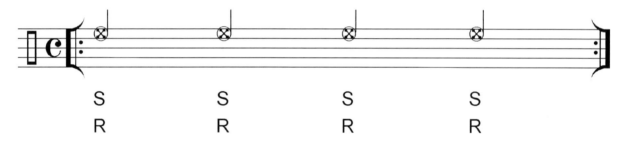

Exercise 5 – DVD Chapter 10

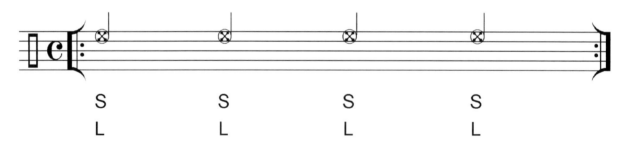

Exercise 6 – DVD Chapter 11

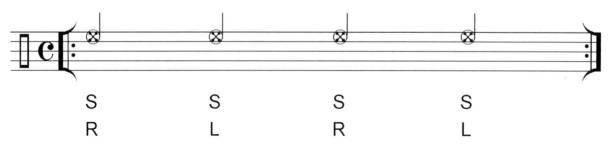

Exercises 7 through 9 introduce the Open Slap. As explained in the previous chapter, the hand position and the stroke itself are the same as the normal slap, but like the open tone the fingers come up off of the skin immediately after the initial impact.

after impact

Exercise 7 – DVD Chapter 12

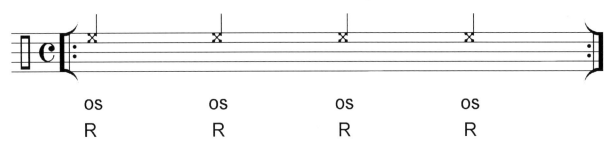

OS	OS	OS	OS
R	R	R	R

Exercise 8 – DVD Chapter 13

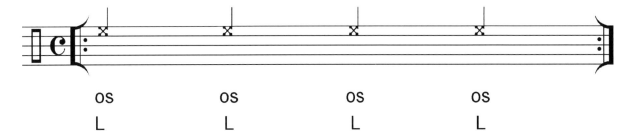

OS	OS	OS	OS
L	L	L	L

Exercise 9 – DVD Chapter 14

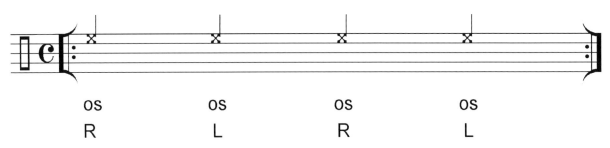

OS	OS	OS	OS
R	L	R	L

Exercise 10 alternates the Open tone with the Closed Slap.

Exercise 10 – DVD Chapter 15

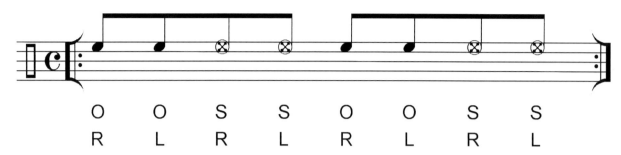

O	O	S	S	O	O	S	S
R	L	R	L	R	L	R	L

Exercise 11 introduces the Bass stroke. The fingers are slightly apart, but the thumb remains tightly closed against the hand. The hand comes down flat in the center of the conga. It's important that the whole hand is used and not just the palm. Outside of Cuba, this stroke is often called the "palm" stroke. The misleading term "heel stroke" is also sometimes used. The importance of using the whole hand will become clear later in the section on "manoteo".

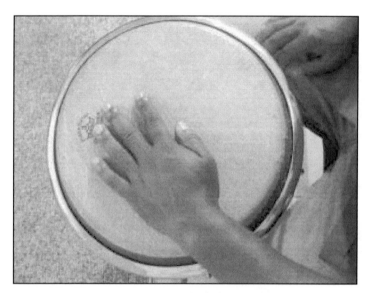

Exercise 11 – DVD Chapter 16

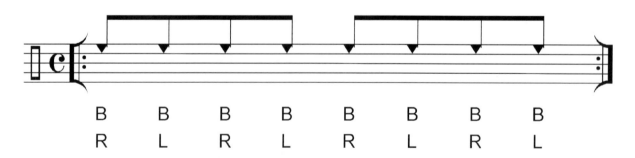

B	B	B	B	B	B	B	B
R	L	R	L	R	L	R	L

Exercises 12 and 13 train you to play different strokes consecutively with the same hand. This may seem illogical at this point, but when you get to the complex 3-drum marchas of Volume III, the necessity for this type of dexterity will become apparent!

Exercise 12 – DVD Chapter 17

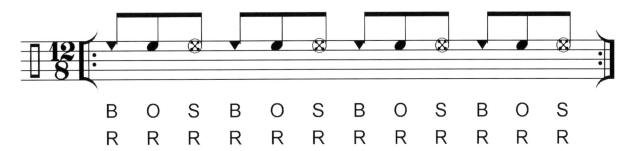

B	O	S	B	O	S	B	O	S	B	O	S
R	R	R	R	R	R	R	R	R	R	R	R

Exercise 13 – DVD Chapter 18

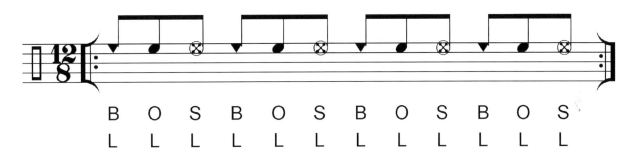

B	O	S	B	O	S	B	O	S	B	O	S
L	L	L	L	L	L	L	L	L	L	L	L

Exercises 14 and 15 review all three of the strokes covered to this point, alternating right and left hands. Remember to start slowly and to make sure each stroke is clear before building up speed.

Exercise 14 – DVD Chapter 19

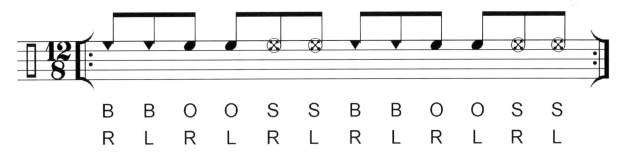

B	B	O	O	S	S	B	B	O	O	S	S
R	L	R	L	R	L	R	L	R	L	R	L

Exercise 15 – DVD Chapter 20

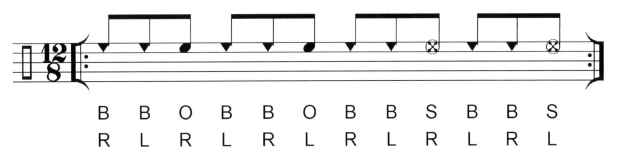

B	B	O	B	B	O	B	B	S	B	B	S
R	L	R	L	R	L	R	L	R	L	R	L

Exercises 16 and 17 introduce the Muff, or *presionado*, stroke. The position of the hands for the Muff stroke is identical to that of the Open stroke, but wheareas the fingers rebound from the skin for the Open stroke, they remain on the skin at the point of impact for the Muff stroke. As indicated by the Spanish term, *presionado*, a slight pressure is added after the stroke to increase the dry and full quality of the muff.

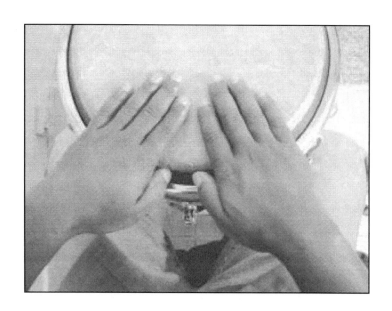

Exercise 16 – DVD Chapter 21

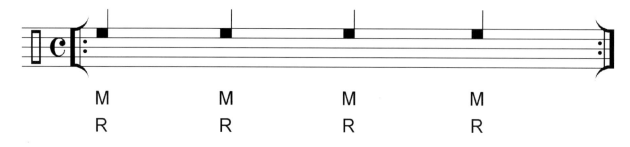

Exercise 17 – DVD Chapter 22

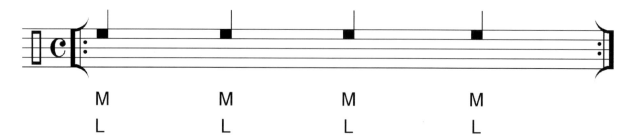

Exercises 18 through 21 combine the Muff and Open strokes in various ways. Note that these strokes are produced with the same motion and on the same part of the drum. The only difference is that the fingers rebound in the Open stroke to let the skin ring out.

Exercise 18 – DVD Chapter 23

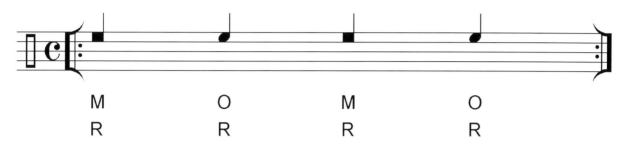

M	O	M	O
R	R	R	R

Exercise 19 – DVD Chapter 24

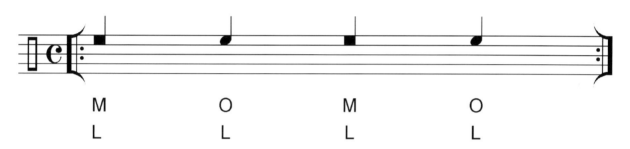

M	O	M	O
L	L	L	L

Exercise 20 – DVD Chapter 25

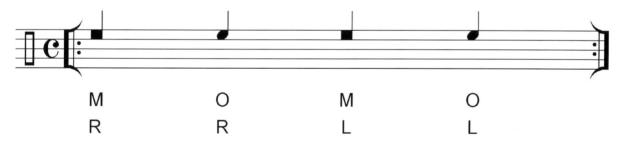

M	O	M	O
R	R	L	L

Exercise 21 – DVD Chapter 26

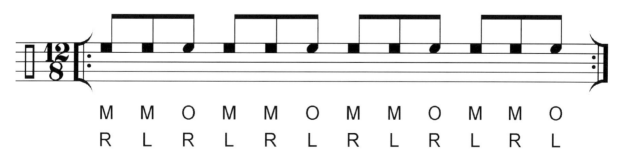

M	M	O	M	M	O	M	M	O	M	M	O
R	L	R	L	R	L	R	L	R	L	R	L

Exercise 22 combines the four strokes covered so far. If you have trouble, review Exericse 15, which is the same as the first half of this exercise.

Exercise 22 – DVD Chapter 27

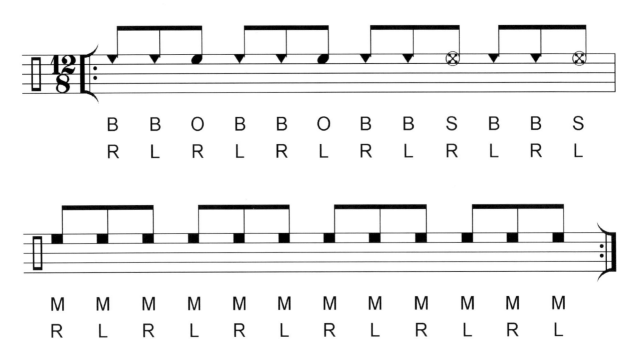

B	B	O	B	B	O	B	B	S	B	B	S
R	L	R	L	R	L	R	L	R	L	R	L

M	M	M	M	M	M	M	M	M	M	M	M
R	L	R	L	R	L	R	L	R	L	R	L

Exercises 23, 24, and 25 introduce the final basic stroke, the Open Slap, used mostly in soloing. The hand position and the stroke itself are the same as the Closed Slap, but like the Open stroke the fingers rebound from the skin immediately after the initial impact.

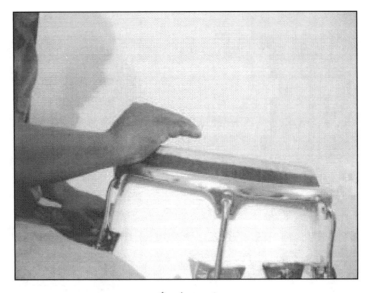

after impact

Exercise 23 – DVD Chapter 28

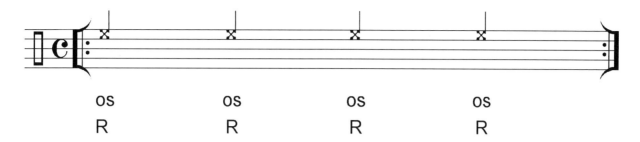

Exercise 24 – DVD Chapter 29

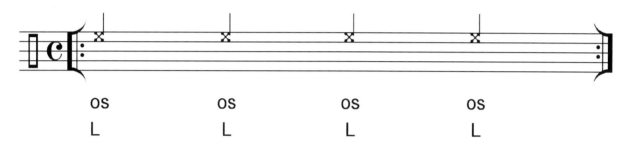

Exercise 25 – DVD Chapter 30

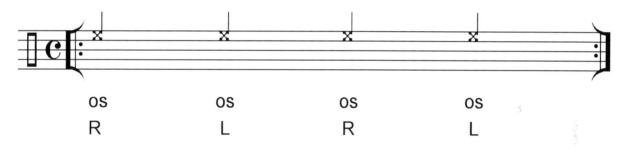

Exercises 26 through 29 combine the Open stroke with the Open Slap in various ways and are an excellent preparation for soloing.

Exercise 26 – DVD Chapter 31

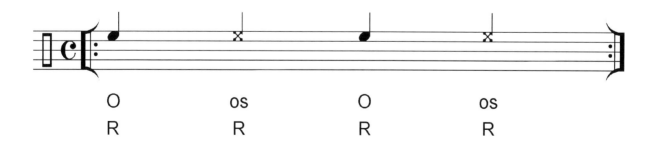

Exercise 27 – DVD Chapter 32

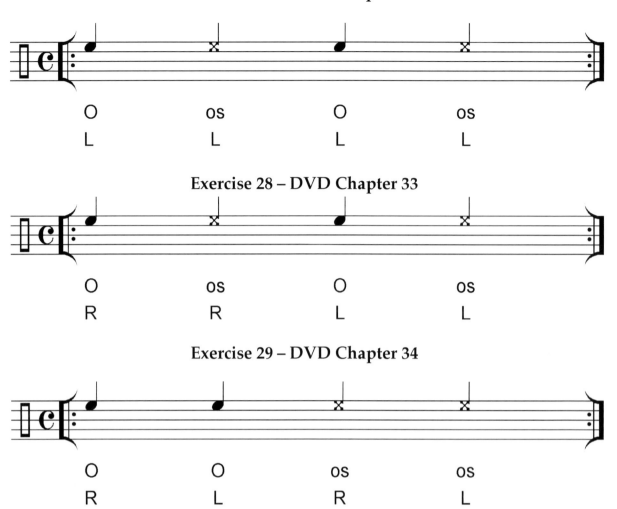

O   os   O   os
L   L   L   L

Exercise 28 – DVD Chapter 33

O   os   O   os
R   R   L   L

Exercise 29 – DVD Chapter 34

O   O   os   os
R   L   R   L

As a final review of all five basic strokes, Exercise 30 alternates Open strokes with each of the other four in succession.

Exercise 30 – DVD Chapter 35

O O B B O O B B O O S S O O S S
R L R L R L R L R L R L R L R L

O O M M O O M M O O os os O O os os
R L R L R L R L R L R L R L R L

34

Group 2: Exercises For the Tip Stroke and Manoteo

TIP (punta)

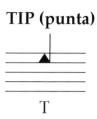

T

The Tip stroke is notated with an upward–pointing triangle to differentiate it from the downward–pointing triangle of the Bass stroke.

(before impact)

The Tip stroke is considered a secondary stroke because it's not a "speaking stroke" in terms of defining the type of rhythm. In folkloric music, because there are usually multiple drummers, sticks, shakers, bells, and other auxiliary percussion, all that is needed to identify a conga rhythm is the "melody" produced by the Open tones, Slaps, and Muffs. Later, with the incorporation of the conga into popular dance music, and with its primary role changed to timekeeping, the Tip stroke was introduced to maintain the time while not getting in the way of other instruments such as the bongó, bass, tres, and maracas.

The Tip stroke employs the same wrist motion and fingertip position as the Closed Slap, but is played in the center of the drum.

In the following exercises, an extremely important timekeeping function of the conga is introduced. This movement is called *manoteo* and consists of two alternating strokes: the Bass and the Tip. Since the manoteo fills in the smallest rhythmic subdivisions of the groove it has to be loud, steady, and crisp. These exercises isolate the technique in order to build proficiency, control and stamina.

In most styles of Latin music, the manoteo is played with the left hand and most of the Slap and Open strokes are played with the right, but in the innovative modern Cuban rhythms covered in Volumes II and III, Open, Slap, and Muff strokes are played on all three drums in endless creative combinations. Thus, for practical reasons, there are many cases where the manoteo has to be transferred to the right hand temporarily to continue to fill in the rhythmic subdivisions necessary for the timing to sound full and steady.

35

A fast, fluid and ambidextrous manoteo is also extremely useful in soloing. For all of these reasons, Exercises 31 through 36 train you to be equally comfortable playing *manoteo* with either hand.

For more on manoteo, see Part 6 and DVD Chapter 59.

Exercises 31 and 32 isolate the manoteo. For left-handed players, the right-handed manoteo will be used most often and vice versa, but be sure to master both.

Exercise 31 – DVD Chapter 36

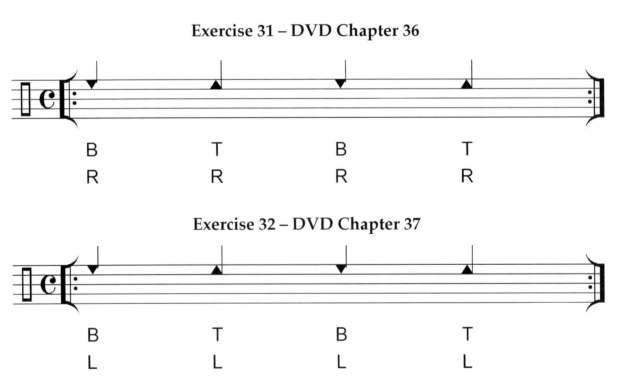

B	T	B	T
R	R	R	R

Exercise 32 – DVD Chapter 37

B	T	B	T
L	L	L	L

Exercises 33 and 34 use an alternating pattern to produce rhythmic displacement between the hands. The right hand manoteo is imitated by the left hand in canon. As Tomasito increases in speed you can hear how effective this type of movement can be for soloing.

Exercise 33 – DVD Chapter 38

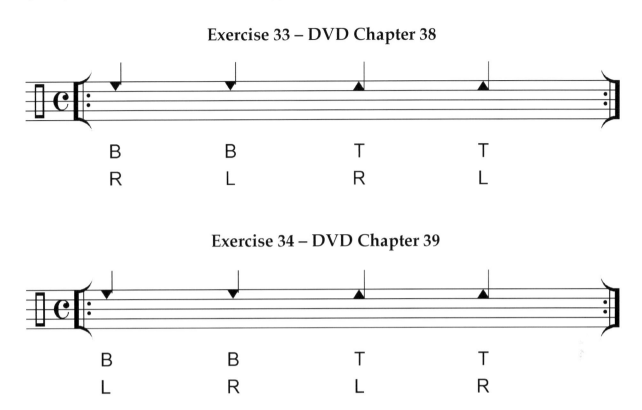

The pattern demonstrated in Exercise 35 is another excellent exercise for developing a crisp manoteo and is also a good soloing device. When this pattern is played beginning with the left Bass stroke as a pickup, it's called *baqueteo de rumba,* the introductory figure played by the congas before the main pattern is established in the Rumba rhythms of *Yambú* and *Guanguancó.* The name is somewhat misleading name because the word *baqueta* (think "baguette") means "drumstick".

Exercise 35 – DVD Chapter 40

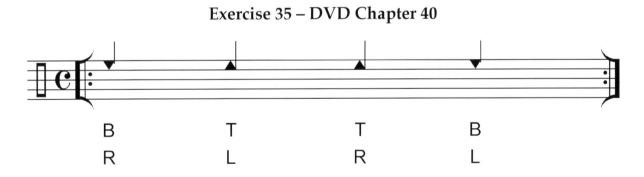

Exercise 36 – DVD Chapter 41 – (see next page for notation)

In Exercise 36, one hand plays a steady manoteo while the other plays twice, then three times, and then four times as fast. This builds independence, stamina, clarity and speed, and it's also extremely important for soloing and for the execution of folkloric rhythms which require the ability to hear and perform duple and triple rhythms simultaneously. In traditional folkloric contexts, each conga is played by a separate musician, but these rhythms are ever more increasingly being adapted to be played by a single conguero on multiple drums.

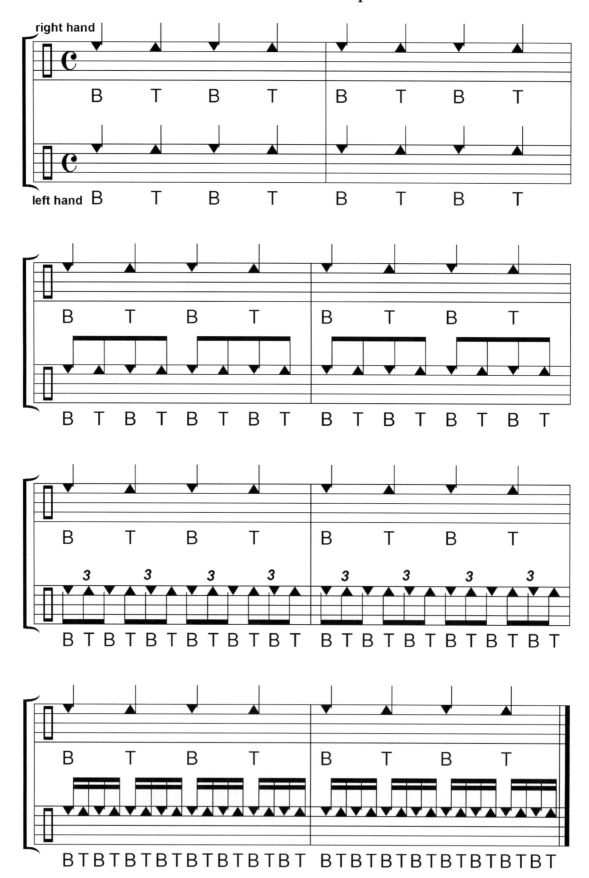

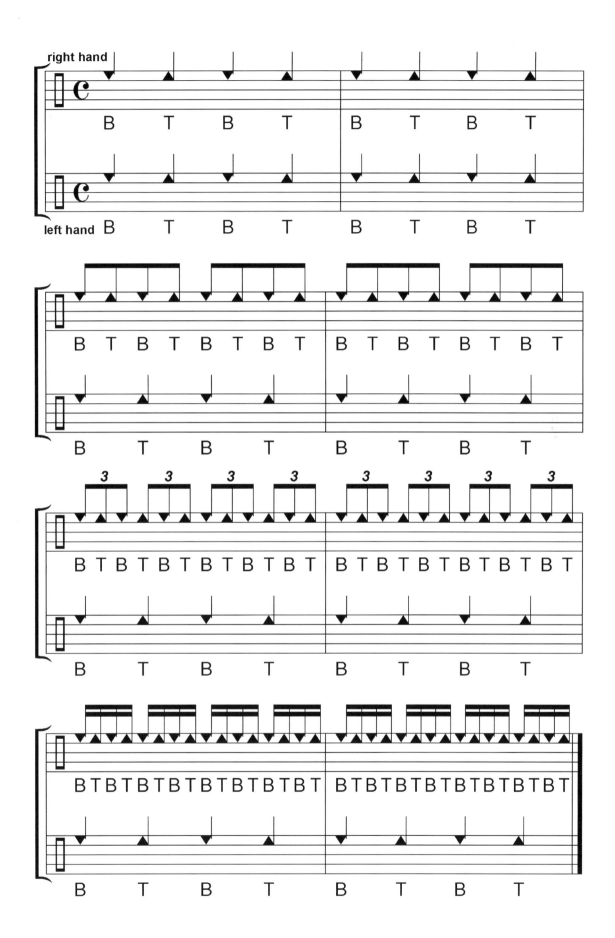

PART 5: RUDIMENTS AND SOLOING

The exercises in Part 5 are powerful tools for developing soloing technique. They're based on "rudiments", a systematic codification of sticking patterns used by trap drummers since the earliest days of military drumming.

The idea of applying these snare drum rudiments to the conga is generally credited to one of Tomasito's teachers, the legendary José Luis "Changuito" Quintana. In addition to being an innovative conguero, Changuito was also an excellent drumset player. In fact, he's best known for playing drums and timbales with the Cuban supergroup, *Los Van Van*. As Changuito explained to coauthor Orlando Fiol, he realized that sticking techniques such as double strokes, ruffs and flams could increase his speed, dexterity and sonic textural variety on congas as well as drums. At that time, the vocabulary of conga soloing was primarily based on the rhythms played by the lead drum in various genres of folkloric music, such as the *quinto* drum in *Rumba*, the *bonkó echemiyá* in *Abacuá*, and the *caja* in *Palo*. Changuito had mastered these folkloric styles, but his mastery of rudiments such as double strokes and flams allowed him to double, triple or even quadruple the speed of the standard solo phrases. As well as playing in Cuba's most famous group, Changuito was and is a tireless teacher and has passed on his technical innovations to hundreds of young Cubans, including Tomás Cruz, as well as visiting musicians such as Giovanni Hidalgo, who went on to take the art of conga soloing to undreamed of levels of virtuosity and creativity. Most recently Changuito has played and arranged for an exciting new Cuban group, *"Pupy Pedroso y Los Que Son Son"*, and has also recently toured the United States and Europe with *Maraca* and other Cuban bands.

One of the most important breakthroughs of rudiments is the introduction of double strokes with the same hand at extremely fast speeds, a practice hitherto reserved for sticks. Changuito and other congueros of the 60's realized that the hand could indeed rebound just as quickly as a stick, but a special flexible technique predicated on wrist movement and finger bouncing had to be developed. Once the fingers can bounce with sufficient strength and volume to produce an open tone or slap comparable in volume and intensity to the same sounds produced with the entire weight of the hand, double stroking is in fact easier because it reduces the necessity for the hand to be raised for each stroke. Double strokes are first practiced at slow speeds using the entire hand as though playing single strokes. This is the default execution of double strokes within the standard conga patterns, or *marchas,* used to keep time, but as the speed increases, it becomes more tense and undesirable to lift the arm or wrist for each stroke, creating a need for the finger-based bounce. The drawback of excessive reliance on finger bounce is that double strokes can sound too weak and soft at fast speeds. Make sure to return to Tomasito's DVD demonstrations frequently as you practice these rudiments to make sure you're producing the correct tone.

Rudiment 1 – DVD Chapter 42

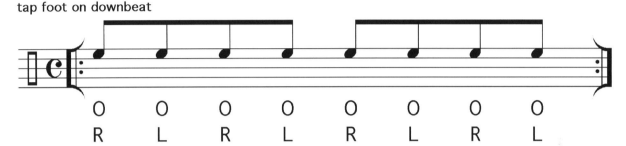

Rudiment 2 – DVD Chapter 43

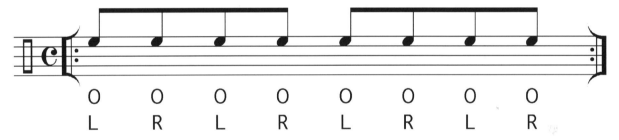

Rudiment 3 – DVD Chapter 44

Rudiment 4 – DVD Chapter 45

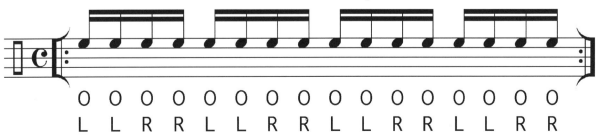

Rudiment 5 – DVD Chapter 46

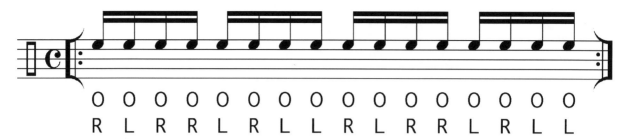

O O O O O O O O O O O O O O O O
R L R R L R L L R L R R L R L L

Rudiment 6 – DVD Chapter 47

O O O O O O O O O O O O O O O O
L R L L R L R R L R L L R L R R

Rudiment 7 – DVD Chapter 48

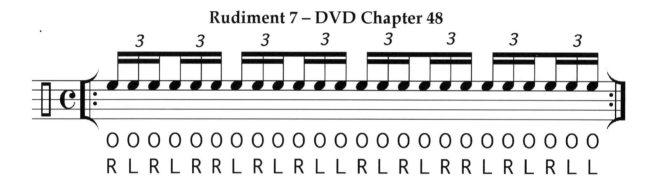

O O O O O O O O O O O O O O O O O O O O O O O O
R L R L R R L R L R L L R L R L R R L R L R L L

Rudiment 8 – DVD Chapter 49

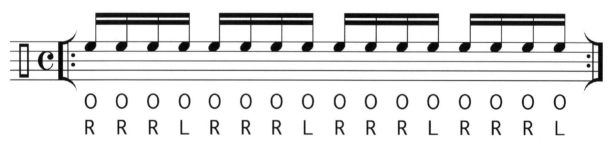

O O O O O O O O O O O O O O O O
R R R L R R R L R R R L R R R L

Rudiment 9 – DVD Chapter 50

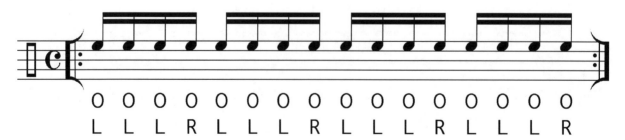

O O O O O O O O O O O O O O O O
L L L R L L L R L L L R L L L R

Rudiment 10 – DVD Chapter 51

O O O O O O O O O O O O O O O O
R R R R L L L L R R R R L L L L

Rudiment 11 – DVD Chapter 52

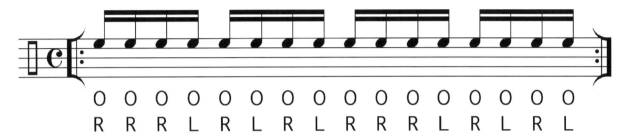

O O O O O O O O O O O O O O O O
R R R L R L R L R R R L R L R L

Rudiment 12 – DVD Chapter 53

O O O O O O O O O O O O O O O O
L L L R L R L R L L L R L R L R

Rudiment 13 – DVD Chapter 54

O O O O O O O O O O O O O O O O
R R L L R L R L R R L L R L R L

Rudiment 14 – DVD Chapter 55

O O O O O O O O O O O O O O O O
L L R R L R L R L L R R L R L R

Rudiment 15 – DVD Chapter 56

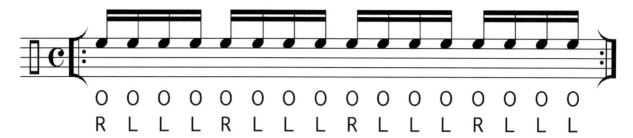

O O O O O O O O O O O O O O O O

R L L L R L L L R L L L R L L L

Rudiment 16 – DVD Chapter 57

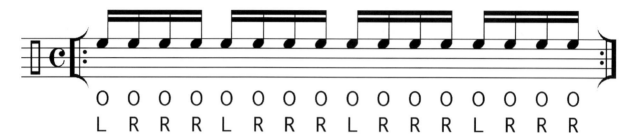

O O O O O O O O O O O O O O O O

L R R R L R R R L R R R L R R R

Rudiment 17 – DVD Chapter 58

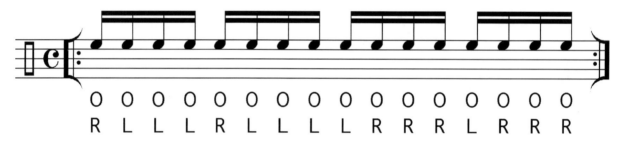

O O O O O O O O O O O O O O O O

R L L L R L L L L R R R L R R R

PART 6: MARCHA EXERCISES

The conguero's most important job is to keep time by playing a repeating pattern of strokes called a *marcha*. A marcha can contain as few as 4 strokes, or, as you'll see in Volume III, as many as 64 strokes before repeating. Most marchas contain no rests – the conguero plays every single rhythmic subdivision. As such it could be said that the conguero is the most important time-keeper in the band. The rhythmic placement of opens and slaps in the conga conga marcha is also an important part of defining the genre being played by the group.

Manoteo

The various types of conga marchas (e.g. *Salsa, Chachachá, Merengue, Timba, Bolero,* etc.), are differentiated by tempo and by the placement of the Open, Slap and Muff tones in the overall rhythmic scheme. For example, the most basic Salsa marcha, often called *tumbao,* goes like this:

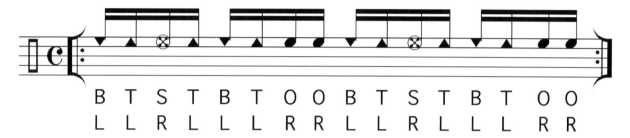

But in the context of the full band playing, what stands out most to the listener is:

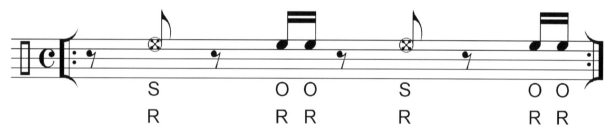

So although the conguero plays all 16 possible rhythmic subdivisions, in this case only six are Slap or Open strokes. The other ten subdivisions are filled with alternating Bass and Tip strokes. This hand movement is called *manoteo.* When you listen to a recording, it's the Slaps and Opens which stand out, but the manoteo is just as important, because it helps to lay down the groove for the conguero as well as for the other musicians on stage. When elements of the band drop out in the breakdown sections that are common in modern Cuban music, the more subtle parts of the conga marcha are exposed and the manoteo gets a chance to take center stage.

Manoteo is a relatively new technique not found in Afro-Cuban folkloric genres such as *Palo, Yuka, Makuta, Iyesá, Bembé,* etc. Exceptions are the modified manoteos which occur in *Rumba Columbia* and *Guaguancó Matancero.* When the conga was adapted to popular music, a single player was expected to approximate the parts which had previously been played by separate players on separate drums, and manoteo was developed to keep the rhythm driving forward between the main strokes.

In most styles, the manoteo is played with the left hand and most of the slaps and opens are played with the right, but the modern Cuban marchas covered in Volume III utilize all strokes and manoteo with both hands in endless creative combinations, so these exercises train you to be equally comfortable playing manoteo with either hand. A fast, fluid and ambidextrous manoteo is also extremely useful in soloing.

In DVD Chapter 59, Tomasito demonstrates the manoteo movement with each hand and then a special two-handed variation used in soloing and also to introduce the afore-mentioned *Rumba Columbia* folkloric rhythm.

Manoteo – DVD Chapter 59

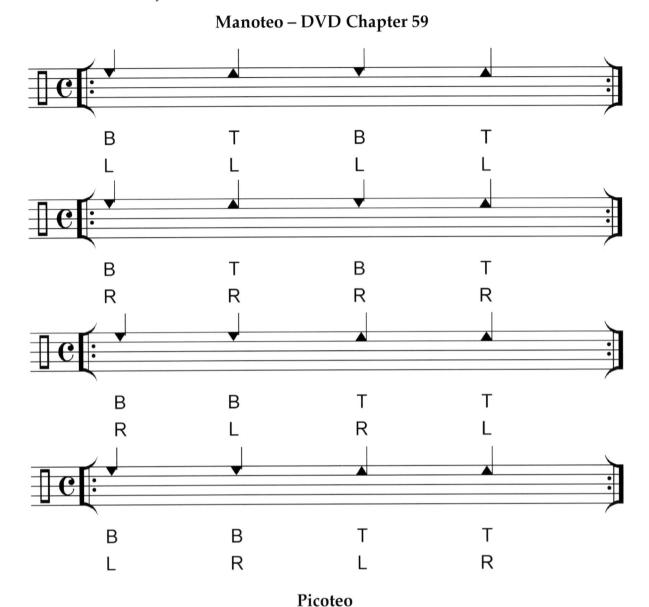

Picoteo

Picoteo, also sometimes called *masacote*, extends the manoteo movement to a four stroke pattern consisting of Bass, Tip, Slap, Tip:

Note that this slap is the "pressed slap" described in Part 2. After playing the first Tip stroke, the left hand remains flat on the drumhead while the Closed Slap is played with the right hand.

The primary goal of the exercises in Part 6 is to develop speed, stamina, and control in the picoteo movement, which is critically important to all forms of popular Cuban music. The exercises involve doubling the manoteo portion and working it up to twice its normal speed.

The first exercise isolates the manoteo movement prior to the Closed Slap. Remember to play each Bass stroke with the full flat hand. One of the most common errors of beginning congueros is to rock the hand in a "heel-tip" motion, resulting in a very weak sounding picoteo. Listen to the fat, full sound of Tomasito's performance on the DVD.

Marcha Exercise 1 – DVD Chapters 60 & 61

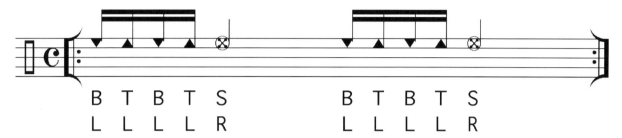

How to Use the Step-by-Step DVD Training Method

This is the first occurence of the special Step-by-Step DVD Method which is used throughout the Tomás Cruz Conga Method series, so let's pause to explain how this powerful practicing tool works.

There are 2 DVD chapters for each marcha covered by the Step-by-Step DVD Method.

In DVD Chapter 60, Tomasito plays Marcha Exercise 1 at full speed. Listen to this a few times until the marcha pattern becomes familiar. Singing along with the full speed DVD chapter is also an excellent idea. Make sure you hear and understand where the clave click track is before proceeding! (See Appendix 1 for an extensive explanation of the clave rhythm).

Now go to DVD Chapter 61. This time the tempo is much slower. Listen carefully to the clave click track and clap along to again make sure you're hearing the clave correctly. Some very famous Timba arrangers have confided to us that they *intentionally* invent ambiguous rhythms which can trick the listener into thinking the downbeat is somewhere other than where it really is! Once you've gotten a rhythm stuck in your head with the wrong orientation it takes four times as long to relearn it the right way, so take our word for it: *always, always, ALWAYS, know where the clave is before you start learning a rhythm!*

Once the clave feels right, you're ready to start the exercise. Set up your congas so you can sit comfortably in front of your television set. Tomasito plays just the first stroke of the pattern, waits for the clave to run its course, and then repeats this cycle for a total of four times. As you watch the DVD, play along. It will be very easy because only one stroke is added at a time and you're given four chances to practice it before the next one is added. A vocal cue announces the next stroke exactly 2 beats before the beginning of the measure that contains the new stroke. The words "quinto" and "tumba" differentiate the small and large drum open tones. A few marchas, such as the one above, repeat after only half a clave, so the process takes half as long.

After four times through, another stroke is added. You may not make it all the way through the exercise the first time, but thanks to the miracle of DVD, you need only press a button to return to the beginning, or to review Chapter 60 to get the sound of the full speed marcha back into your ear. At the first sign of frustration, just start over. *Don't worry about how long it takes* – just keep your level of frustration completely under control by starting over whenever necessary.

Learning complex marchas, such as the Timba marchas in Volume III, doesn't have to be hard if you only add one new note at a time. The whole idea of this exercise is that it's supposed to be easy. As soon as you feel yourself "trying", grab that remote control and start the exercise over. Remember that what you're learning subconsciously from staring at Tomasito's hands is *more* important than learning the pattern itself – it's the nuances of rhythm, tone and feeling that make his recordings and performances so satisfying and by practicing along with the DVD each day you'll begin to absorb these qualities into your own playing. The feeling of "swing" is difficult or impossible to explain in words, and there's no doubt that the best, if not the *only* way to learn it is the way Tomás himself learned it – by "osmosis". In Cuba, these subtleties are handed down from generation to generation by example – not by explanation – and you can use the DVD to let Tomasito hand a little of his magic down to you.

Play along with DVD Chapter 61 every day until you can play the full pattern effortlessly enough to start practicing with the full speed version, DVD Chapter 60.

The Term "Quinto"

In the vocal cues on the DVD we use the terms *"quinto"* and *"tumba"* for the smaller and larger of the two drums. These are sometimes also called *"macho"* and *"hembra"*. To avoid any possible confusion, note that in Rumba, *quinto* refers to the lead drum, which is sometimes even smaller than the smallest drum used in popular music. The Rumba quinto is used only for soloing and never plays marchas because of its higher pitch.

When there is a third, middle drum, as in Volume III, we use the term *"tres dos"*.

✳ ✳ ✳

Marcha Exercises 2 through 5 concentrate on the transition from the Slap to the Tip. The sequence of Slap, Tip, Bass, Tip occurs in most marchas. For each Marcha, there are 2 DVD Chapters, one at full speed and asecond either in slow motion or with the Step-by-Step DVD Method.

Marcha Exercise 2 – DVD Chapters 62 & 63

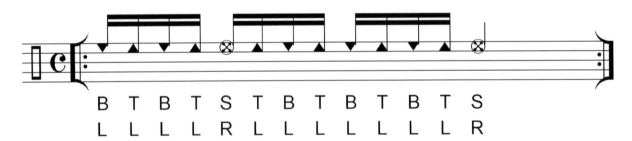

Marcha Exercise 3 – DVD Chapter 64 & 65

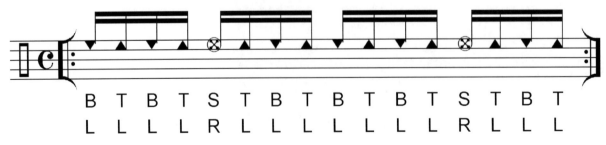

Marcha Exercise 4 – DVD Chapter 66 & 67

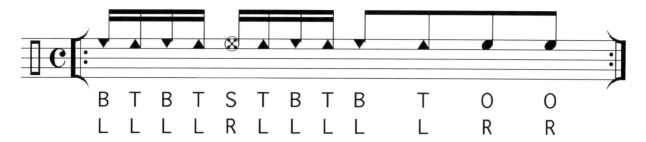

B T B T S T B T B   T   O   O
L L L L R L L L L   L   R   R

Marcha Exercise 5 – DVD Chapter 68 & 69

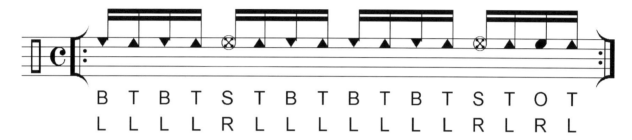

B T B T S T B T B T B T B T S T O T
L L L L R L L L L L L L L L R L R L

Marcha Exercise 6 isolates the picoteo motion itself.

Marcha Exercise 6 – DVD Chapter 70 & 71

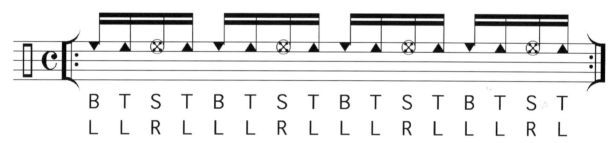

B T S T B T S T B T S T B T S T
L L R L L L R L L L R L L L R L

Tomasito with drummer Yoel Páez and trombonist Julio Montalvo on tour with the Cuban supergroup Paulito FG y su Élite in Cancún, 1997.

Julio, Leo, Yoel, Tomasito
Photos courtesy of Yoel Páez (http://yoelpaez.timba.com)

Marcha Exercise 7 incorporates all of the other exercises in Part 6 into one lengthy arrangement. Tomasito suggests memorizing it and using it as a warmup before practicing or performing. Start out slowly and gradually build up speed.

Marcha Exercise 7 – DVD Chapter 72

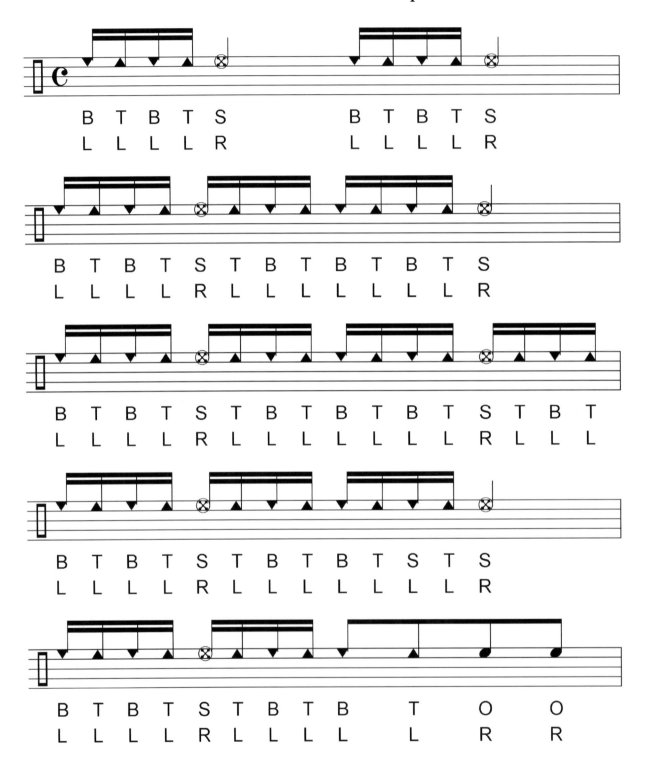

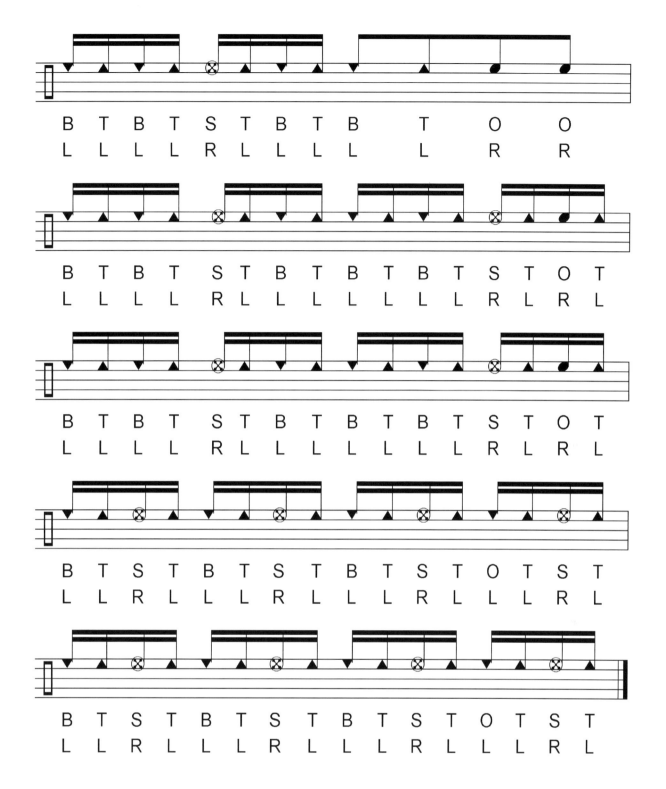

51

PART 7: MARCHAS

Part 7 contains an assortment of easy marchas that should be sufficient to get you through a basic Latin gig or jam session. After mastering these, you'll be ready to move on to Volume II, which covers a wide range of marchas such as *Songo, Merengue, Guaguancó, Iyesá, Cumbia, Bomba, Pilón, Afro, Suku–Suku, Dengue, Mozambique, 6/8,* etc. Volume III covers the *Timba* marchas and rhythm sections "gears" which have accompanied the latest surge in musical creativity that has taken place in Cuba from 1990 to the present.

Marcha 1 – Marcha Cerrada – DVD Chapters 73 & 74

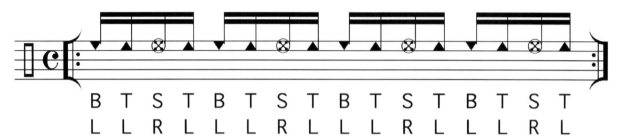

Marcha 1 is sometimes called *marcha cerrada,* or "closed marcha", because it has no open tones. – it simply repeats the Picoteo pattern four times. It's an excellent choice for introductions, breakdowns, and other sections where the conguero wants to keep strong time without playing loudly or obtrusively. In this case, DVD Chapter 74 is played at a slow tempo rather than using the Step-by-Step method. Throughout this 3-volume set, each marcha will have two DVD chapters and use one of these techniques to help you study it.

Marcha 2 – Tumbao (one drum) – DVD Chapters 75 & 76

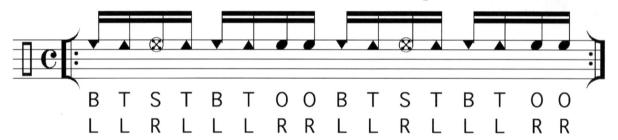

Marcha 2 is the most generic form of *the* most common conga marcha, originally introduced by Arsenio Rodríguez in the 1940's. Rodríguez is also generally credited with being the first to use the conga in a popular music setting. This pattern and variations of it are sometimes referred to simply as *"tumbao"*.

To understand why this pattern fits so naturally in Latin popular music, let's take a look at the pattern of another of the most important time-keepers of the rhythm section, the *cencerro* bell, sometimes called the *campana* or bongo bell. Its pattern is called *campaneo*.

2-3 Campaneo

The cencerro plays a loud open bell tone on each downbeat of the measure. Now let's look at Marcha 2 with the manoteo removed:

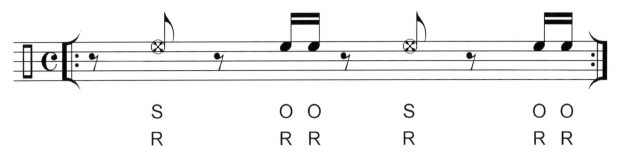

The conga acts as a counterweight to the cencerro, with the two slaps and the two double open figures occupying each upbeat of the measure. The click track that Tomasito uses in the DVD chapter consists of the four main cencerro tones and the clave. As you practice along with the DVD, note that main strokes of your pattern come at the halfway points between the main beats as played by the open cencerro bell. You can also practice tapping your foot on the downbeats.

Marcha 3 – DVD Chapters 77 & 78

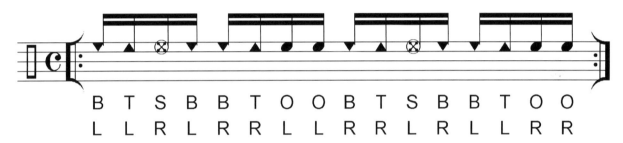

Marcha 3 looks and sounds a lot like Marcha 2 until you start to play it and realize that while the second half *sounds* just like the first, it's played with the opposite hands. If you have difficulty, start by learning Marcha 2 with the handing reversed, as a left-handed conguero would play it. Marcha 3 forces you to switch from a right-handed to a left-handed orientation every 2 beats. However, once you master it, you'll be surprised to discover that you can actually play it faster because at no point do you have to play three strokes in a row with the same hand, as you do in Marcha 2. In Volume III, when you're using 3 drums, you'll find this ability to free up the opposite hand by using two consecutive bass strokes to be very useful.

Marcha 4 – Tumbao (2 drums) – DVD Chapters 79 & 80

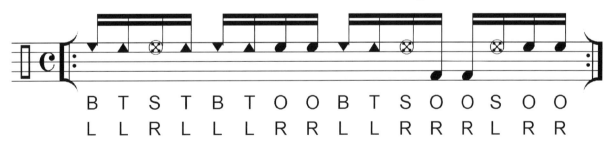

After Marcha 2, Marcha 4 is probably the second most common conga marcha, and the first time in this book that the *tumba,* or low drum, is used. Tumba strokes are notated with the same type of noteheads, but they're written on the bottom space instead of the top. Almost of all of the marchas in Volume II use two drums and many of those in Volume III add the *tres dos,* or middle drum, which, for future reference, is notated on the middle line.

Marcha 4 also marks the first point in this book that it becomes necessary to discuss what is perhaps the most important, compelling, and sometimes confounding aspect of Latin music: *clave*. Appendix 1 provides a thorough introduction to clave and we'll delve even deeper into the subject in Volumes II & III. For now, however, just pay close attention to the clave click track on the DVD as you practice Marcha 4.

Chachachá

The *chachachá* owes its origins to the *Danzón*, a courtly European-influenced Cuban genre that was popular in the early 20th century. Danzones would typically begin with a less syncopated, more elegant, melodic section before going into a funkier, more danceable second half called the *estribillo,* which became the basis for the chachachá rhythm which became extremely popular in later decades in the hands of such artists as Cachao. Today the chachachá is still played quite frequently in both dance and Latin Jazz settings. It's usually played slower than Salsa and Timba.

After studying the section on clave in Appendix 1, you'll see that Marchas 5 & 6, like Marchas 2 & 4, are similar except for the use of the big drum on the 3-side of the clave. Also note that the clave on the DVD click track is Son clave as opposed to the Rumba clave used for Marchas 1 through 4.

Marcha 5 – Chachachá (one drum) – DVD Chapters 81 & 82

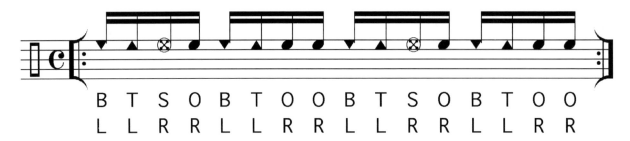

Marcha 6 – Chachachá (two drums) – DVD Chapters 83 & 84

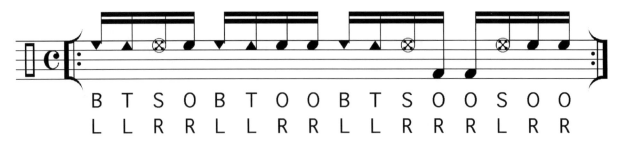

Marcha 7 – Bolero – DVD Chapters 85 & 86

B T S T B O O O B T S T B O O O
L L R L L R L R L L R L L R L R

The *bolero* rhythm is used for slow ballads. Because bolero, largely of European origin, has no clave orientation, the DVD chapters use a different type of click track using the *cáscara de bolero* rhythm played by the maracas or on the shell of the timbale drum.

PART 8: RECURSOS

Like any other instrumentalist, the conguero inherits, and hopefully adds to, an arsenal or vocabulary of characteristic "licks" which can be used as fills during exciting sections of songs, or as transitional material between the more spontaneously improvised phrases of solos. In Spanish, these licks are called *recursos.* When playing recursos, the conguero's job is to distinguish himself from the rhythmic orientation of the rest of the rest of the band. This is done with various combinations of syncopation and double, triple, quadruple, sextuple or even octuple time. To further call attention to the congas, recursos are designed to be "noisy", employing the loudest conga strokes: open tones, open slaps and double strokes with both hands.

Recurso 1 – DVD Chapter 87

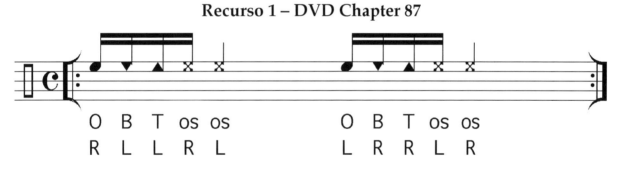

O B T os os   O B T os os
R L L R L   L R R L R

Recurso 2 – DVD Chapter 88

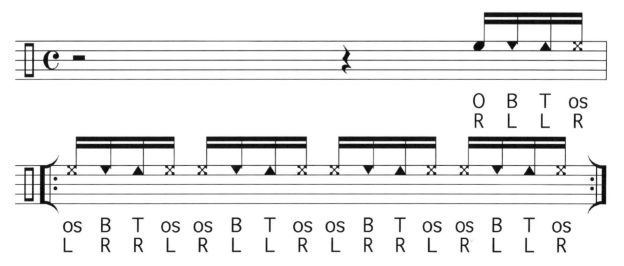

O B T os
R L L R

os B T os os B T os os B T os os B T os
L R R L R L L R L R R L R L L R

normal marcha

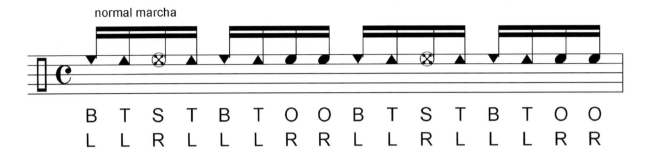

B T S T B T O O B T S T B T O O
L L R L L L R R L L R L L L R R

exit from marcha   recurso

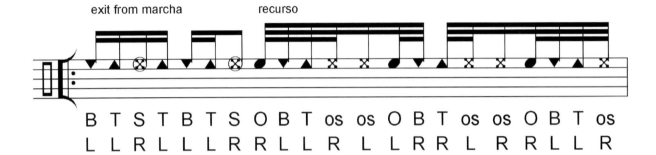

B T S T B T S O B T os os O B T os os O B T os
L L R L L L L R R L L R L L R R L R R L L R

return to marcha

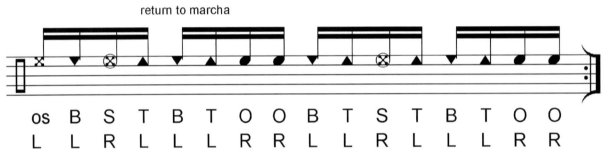

os B S T B T O O B T S T B T O O
L L R L L L R R L L R L L L R R

Tomasito live in Miami with
Manolín, el Médico de la Salsa – 2002
(photo courtesy of Duniel Deya)

56

normal marcha

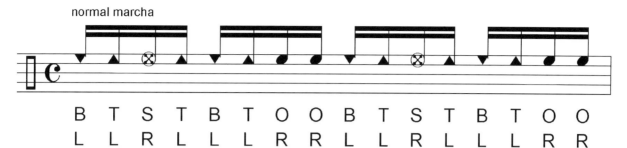

B	T	S	T	B	T	O	O	B	T	S	T	B	T	O	O
L	L	R	L	L	L	R	R	L	L	R	L	L	L	R	R

exit from marcha   recurso

B	T	S	T	B	T	S	O	B	T	os	os	B	T	os	os	B	T	os	os	B	T	os
L	L	R	L	L	L	R	R	L	L	R	L	R	R	L	R	L	L	R	L	R	R	L

return to marcha

os	B	S	T	B	T	O	O	B	T	S	T	B	T	O	O
L	L	R	L	L	L	R	R	L	L	R	L	L	L	R	R

All recording session photos by Tom Ehrlich.

APPENDIX 1: CLAVE

Part 1: Introduction

Clave is one of the most important, compelling, and sometimes confusing aspects of studying Latin music. To Cuban musicians like Tomasito, the clave rhythm is as natural as breathing, and like breathing, is something that simply doesn't require intellectual analysis. It's just a fact of life. Clave to a Cuban musician is like the backbeat snare drum is to an American musician. You can play it, vary it, play against it, or leave it out all together, but the feeling of it, like gravity, is always unmistakably and undeniably present.

But to those students of Latin music who are not so lucky as to have been born with "clave in the blood", the term has an altogether different significance. To them, trying to learn to feel and understand the clave is akin to the quest for the Holy Grail. On the one hand, the more you study clave, the easier and more natural playing Latin music becomes, but at the same time, the more you learn, the more you'll realize there *is* to learn about clave.

Part 2 of this section provides you with the essential information about clave that you need to study Volume I while avoiding too much confusing detail. Part 3 goes into greater detail, looking ahead to the challenges of Volumes II & III, and finally, Part 4 deals with some of the apparent contradictions in terminology and notation which have left Latin music students pulling out their collective hair for decades. Remember that for the study of Volume I, Part 2 is all you really need to understand.

Part 2: Essential Information About Clave for Volume I

Clave is a 5–stroke repeating rhythm pattern which is present or implied in most Latin music. There are various types of clave but the only two used in Volume I are what we call "2-3 Son Clave" and "2-3 Rumba Clave". The Marcha Exercises and Marchas 1 through 4 (DVD Chapters 60 through 80) use 2-3 Rumba clave and Marchas 5 & 6 (DVD Chapters 81-84) use 2-3 Son Clave. In Parts 3 & 4, we'll discuss the widespread disagreement and confusion about the *names* of these rhythms, but for now let's just agree to use these two terms and listen to rhythms.

Listen to the beginning of DVD Chapter 73. The bell comes right on the beat and the other sound is the clave:

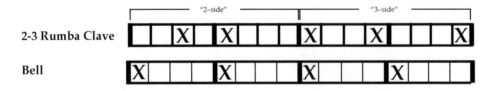

Now listen to the beginning of DVD Chapter 81. The only difference is that the last note of the clave comes one subdivision earlier:

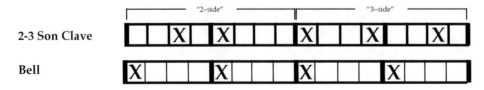

It's important to note that the marcha exercises and Marchas 1-4, which are recorded with a Rumba Clave click track, would work just as well with Son Clave, but Marchas 5 & 6, both chachachás, would generally *not* be played with Rumba Clave.

For the conguero studying Volume I, a comprehensive understanding of clave is much less important than developing the following two abilities:

1) <u>Be able to clap the clave while you listen to the marcha.</u>

2) <u>Be able to play the marcha while you listen to the clave.</u>

Part 3: Towards a Deeper Understanding of Clave

To understand the role of clave as a governing principle in rhythm, let's start by separating it from two other governing principles which are independent of the clave: the beat, and the subdivisions of the beat.

The Beat: Put on your favorite recording and tap your foot along with the music. Depending on the song, this tapping might be slower or faster, but the taps, like heartbeats, always come at regular intervals. The speed of these "beats" is called the "tempo". Now put on DVD Chapter 73 and tap your foot along with the bell. The bell is playing the beat. DVD Chapter 74 is a slower performance of the same marcha. In both cases, the bell plays the beat – only the tempo changes. In each case, make sure that you don't find yourself tapping your foot twice as fast as the bell, a common beginner's mistake. As you listen to and play various types of Latin dance music you'll frequently hear the beat played on this same type of bell, called the *campana* or *cencerro*. It's traditionally hand-held and played by the bongocero, but in modern Cuban music it's sometimes mounted on a stand and played by either the timbalero or the trap drummer. In most cases, the campana pattern, or *campaneo*, is decorated with additional, higher pitched strokes played on the heel of the bell. How these strokes are chosen is very definitely determined by the clave, but the steady flow of open bell tones is independent of the clave. The DVD click tracks use just the open bell tones, giving you the beat in its purest form.

The Subdivisions of the Beat: Depending on the style of music, each beat may be subdivided into 2, 3, 4, or more subdivisions. Like the beats themselves, these subdivisions come at regular intervals. For example, rock & roll usually has two subdivisions per beat, while a blues shuffle has three and funk, rap and hip–hop usually have four. The great majority of popular Latin rhythms have four subdivisions per beat, although Afro–Cuban folkloric rhythms (see Volume II), can have three or four subdivisions and in some cases both simultaneously! Also, like hip-hop and jazz, some of these folkloric rhythms place certain strokes *between* the 1/3 and 1/4 subdivisions, creating an effect sometimes called "swing". Keeping this idea of subdivisions in mind, listen again to DVD Chapter 73 and notice that the conga marcha consists of exactly four evenly-spaced strokes for each beat of the bell. To hear this in slow motion, listen to DVD Chapter 74. Now scan through some of the other marchas you've studied, noting that in every case, the conga marcha consists of all four subdivisions of each beat, with none left out and nothing else added. The conga is the only instrument in the popular Latin ensemble which consistently plays all the subdivisions (except of course during solos).

To summarize, the principal job of the bell player is to state the beat and yours, as the conguero, is to state the subdivisions of the beat. Both of these functions are independent of the clave.

Listen once again to DVD Chapters 73 & 74, being conscious of the bell playing the beat and the conga playing the subdivisions. What's left is the clave itself.

The Clave: The clave pattern consists of 5 strokes asymmetrically arranged across 4 beats, or across a total of 16 subdivisions. Leaving aside the folkloric rhythms of Volume II that use 3 subdivisions per beat, there are four clave patterns that the conguero will encounter:

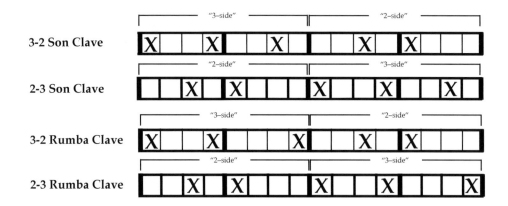

Note that the terms "3-side" and "2-side" are derived from the amount of strokes in each 2-beat section and that the "3-2" and "2-3" versions of each clave are really the same rhythm starting on a different "side". We'll explain some of the confusion about these two subjects in Part 4.

Clave and the Instruments of the Latin Ensemble: The rhythm patterns of each instrument in the Latin ensemble are influenced by the clave. It's very important for the conguero to know the parts of the other percussionists and how they relate to the clave.

The clave rhythm itself can be played with two sticks (also called claves), but is more often played by the timbalero or trap drummer on a plastic woodblock-like instrument known as a "jam block". Sometimes the clave rhythm is not played at all, but the musicians and informed listeners can still hear where the 2-side and 3-side are by listening to the parts of the other instruments, which imply the clave just as strongly.

The following examples are shown starting on the 2-side of the clave. 2-3 Rumba Clave is shown as a reference, but the patterns would be the same when played against 2-3 Son Clave. The key point is that the 2-side of the pattern must stay in sync with the 2-side of the clave.

Campaneo: The campana or cencerro bell states the beat with open tones ("O") and marks the clave with the heel ("H") of the bell. An accented single "H", on the 2-side imitates the clave.

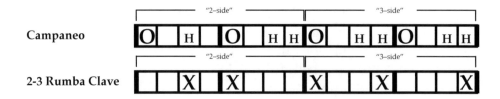

Contracampaneo: The *contracampana*, or "mambo bell", or "timbale bell" pattern is played on a smaller mounted bell by either the timbalero or trap drummer. It also clearly accents the 2-side and has a characteristically more-syncopated rhythm on the 3-side.

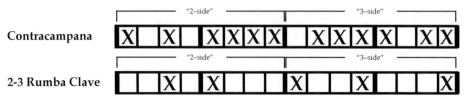

Cáscara: The *cáscara* rhythm is usually played on the side, or shell, of the higher timbale drum, and also sometimes on the ride cymbal.

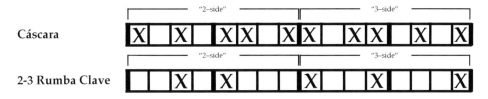

The parts of the piano, bass, horns, voices, kick drum and congas vary greatly from style to style and from arrangement to arrangement, but they, like everything in Latin music, are always affected by the presence of the clave. There are even cases, especially with the kick drum and more complex conga marchas, where an instrument intentionally plays *"contraclave"*, or "against the clave". Such an example is the *Guaguancó* rhythm where the open conga tones outline the 3-side against the 2-side of the clave! The "gravitational force" of the clave is always present, but how creative arrangers and musicians deal with that force leaves a lot of room for artistic discretion.

Clave and Conga Marchas:

Now let's take a look at the relationship between the clave and some of the marchas we've already studied. For these examples, we'll show only the first letter of the name of each stroke, using a lower-case "o" for the open stroke on the smaller "quinto" drum and an upper-case "O" for the open stroke on the larger "tumba" drum.

First let's look at Marchas 1, 2, 3, and 5:

Marcha 1   `B T S T B T S T B T S T B T S T`

Marcha 2   `B T S T B T o o B T S T B T o o`

Marcha 3   `B T S B B T o o B T S B B T o o`

Marcha 5   `B T S o B T o o B T S o B T o o`

2-3 Rumba Clave   `. . X . X . . X . X . . X`

2-3 Son Clave   `. . X . X . . X . X . X .`

Note that in Marchas 2, 3, and 5 the pattern repeats after 8 strokes, and in Marcha 1, it repeats after only 4. It follows that you wind up playing exactly the same sequence of strokes on the 2-side as you do against the 3-side. These marchas are perfect for use in under-rehearsed gigs and jam sessions when you don't know in advance what the clave is. You can play these "safe marchas" until the direction of the clave becomes clear and then switch to something more adventurous.

Now let's look at Marchas 4 & 6:

Marcha 4

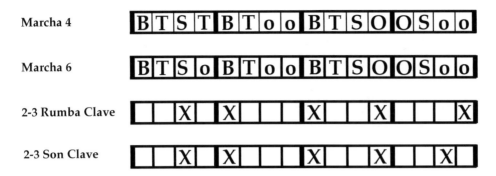

Marcha 6

2-3 Rumba Clave

2-3 Son Clave

These marchas, like the clave itself, continue for 16 subdivisions before repeating, and are traditionally played so that the two open tumba tones are played on the 3-side. This is called "playing the big drum on the 3-side", an interesting convention discussed further in Part 4. When playing an arrangement that's "in 3-2" (also see Part 4), you would invert these marchas like this:

Marcha 4 in 3-2

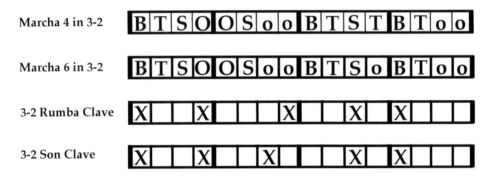

Marcha 6 in 3-2

3-2 Rumba Clave

3-2 Son Clave

The relationship between clave and marcha is of paramount importance, so study the two diagrams above until you're certain you completely understand them! If you have any doubts, feel free to email us at **kevin@timba.com**. We'll be happy to clarify anything that doesn't make sense.

Part 4: Clave Confusion Stemming from Terminology and Notation

Even the best percussionists can often be heard arguing endlessly about the terms and concepts surrounding the elusive subject of clave. It's a great understatement to say that "clave is something that should be felt, and not talked about!" But clave's "Catch-22" is that unless you were born hearing it, you have to go through a sometimes painful period of trying to understand it well enough to teach yourself to feel it and there are some nasty roadblocks standing in the way of those trying to understand it!

Here are some of the most common:

1) 8th notes versus 16th notes
2) "3-2 clave" versus "2-3 clave"
3) "Son Clave" versus "Rumba Clave"
4) "Playing the big drum on the 3-side"
5) "Clave Changes" and "Jumping the Clave"

Let's tackle them one by one:

8th notes versus 16th notes

In Cuba, music is usually written in 16th notes such that one clave lasts one measure of 4/4, but outside of Cuba, music is usually written in 8th notes such that one clave lasts two measures. Most instructional books on the market also use the 8th note method.

Here are 3 ways of writing the same rhythm, 3-2 Rumba Clave:

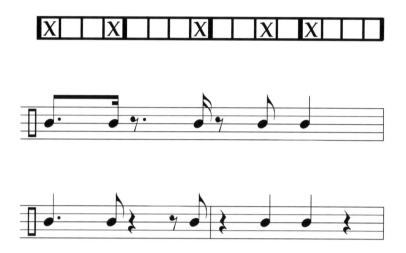

The "box" diagram at the top is the least ambiguous, showing the 4 main beats, each with 4 subdivisions, for a total of 16 possible locations, of which the clave occupies 5. Of the other two, the 16th note diagram really makes more sense because it shows the rhythm over the space of 4 quarter notes, and, in common time, or 4/4, a quarter note gets one beat. If you were to take the 8th note diagram literally, you would conclude that one clave lasts 8 beats, each with 2 subdivisions, which, as we pointed out above, is completely wrong and will result in a beginner feeling the clave incorrectly. Nevertheless, unless you live in Cuba, almost all the written Latin music you encounter will be written in 8th notes and you will simply be expected to know that you have to think in 2/2, or "cut time" so that you still are only feeling 4 beats per clave. The advantage of this method is that the page looks less cluttered and many professional musicians find it much easier to read. Also, your eye doesn't have to decipher the double-flagged sixteenth notes and sixteenth rests, or the dotted rests.

To please everyone, we supply both types of notation, with the 8th note versions in a special appendix. In a close call, we chose the 16th note method for the main text to be sure that beginners understand that a clave lasts 4 beats, not 8.

Of course, many of the best professional congueros don't even know how to read music and play by ear. As we pointed out in the introduction, if you yourself don't know how to read music, you've probably discovered that it's very easy to "read" the exercises in this book by simply looking at the letters beneath the notes.

Note: The earliest examples of notation in Cuba were written in 16th notes, but in 2/4, such that the clave lasted 2 bars, but the beat was still accurately represented.

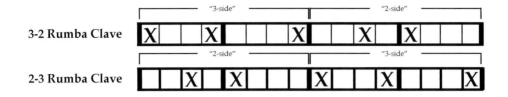

These are really the same rhythm, starting in different places. The only difference is where you start counting "1, 2, 3, 4", or, in 16th note notation, where the barlines are.

If you walked into a room where someone had already begun playing clave, you wouldn't be able to say whether it was "3-2" or "2-3" because the clave rhythm is a repeating loop and you wouldn't know where the person had started, or where the person was imagining the barlines to be. However, if the piano, bass, voices and horns were to come in and make it clear where the barlines were, you could then say that musical piece was "in 2-3" or "in 3-2".

Or could you? Most of the time, it's quite obvious where the barlines are when you hear the whole band playing together, but sometimes, because of the nature of pickups, it's actually possible that even with the whole band playing, two listeners could perceive the barline as being in different places. Furthermore, some Cuban music has intentionally ambiguous over-lapping phrases such that one instrument might seem to be putting its "barlines" on one side of the clave while another puts them on the other side! If this seems far-fetched, try this experiment: get a group of musicians or Latin music fans together to listen to recordings, asking each person to show where he or she hears the "1, 2, 3, 4", especially during the "coro" sections that are found in the second halves of the arrangements. Some interesting choices might be *"¿Y ahora qué?"* by Paulito FG, *"Extraños ateos"* by David Calzado y La Charanga Habanera, and *"Güiro, calabaza, y miel"* by Manolito y su Trabuco. You may be surprised to discover that often a section which sounds like it's obviously in 3-2 to you will sound like it's in 2-3 to someone else.

The only way to be 100% sure whether you're in 3-2 or 2-3 is to actually look at the written chart and see where the barlines are written and even this would only work if the chart were written in 16th notes, because in 8th notes there's a separate bar for each "side" of the clave. This is another argument in favor of writing music in 16th notes. Since each clave takes only one mea-sure, the arranger is forced to reveal how he or she hears the "1, 2, 3, 4".

But some bands, such as Bamboleo, don't even use charts – even the horn players learn their parts by ear in rehearsal. Because the only difference between "2-3" and "3-2" is where one subjectively hears the barlines, it's even theoretically possible for two musicians in the same band to have their clave-based parts in sync while each perceives the musical phrases of the arrangement as beginning on different sides! And as we pointed out earlier, sometime arrang-ers intentionally set the instruments off against each other for artistic reasons. In short, written music with its time signatures and barlines is sometimes simply not adequate to represent the complex rhythms of some Cuban music and while the concept of "2-3" and "3-2" is very prac-tical and useful in most cases, it has also has inherent potential for causing mass confusion.

So what's a poor conguero to do? Not to worry. It doesn't matter where *you* subjectively per-ceive the "1, 2, 3, 4" as long as the 2-side of your marcha lines up with the 2-side of the clave and the 3-side of your marcha lines up with the 3-side of the clave. In the case of Marchas 1, 2, 3, 5, and 7, the marcha pattern is the same on both sides of the clave, so you couldn't get it wrong if you tried, but if you're using a marcha which is different on each side of the clave (e.g. Marcha 4 or 6), you have to be able to hear where the clave is and make your part line up with it. Fortunately, when in doubt, you can always just play Marcha 2 until you figure out where the clave is.

Son Clave versus Rumba Clave

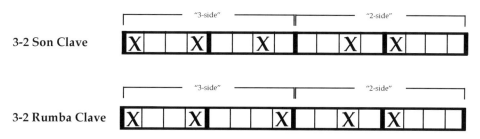

As we've already discussed, the only difference between Son and Rumba Clave is that the third note of the 3-side comes one subdivision later in Rumba Clave, creating a more syncopated rhythm. Some genres (e.g. *Guaguancó*) and some groups (e.g. La Charanga Habanera) use Rumba Clave exclusively while others use Son Clave exclusively. Still others (e.g. Issac Delgado, Los Van Van, Klimax) switch from section to section and many groups will in fact alternate back and forth between Son & Rumba Clave almost randomly within the same section. To hear such an example, listen to the legendary studio recording of NG La Banda's "Santa Palabra". Even the more traditional group Orquesta Aragón sometimes switches between Son & Rumba Clave in the middle of the same coro section. So while a *guaguancó* should always use Rumba Clave and a *chachachá* should always use Son Clave, there are also many cases where either or both can be used, so it's necessary to avoid being too rigid about the distinction between these two rhythms.

For example, in this volume, note that the DVD click tracks for Marchas 5 & 6 use Son Clave, while Marchas 1-4 use Rumba Clave. It's very unlikely that chachachá marchas like Marchas 5 & 6 would ever use Rumba Clave, but any of Marchas 1-4 could just as easily be played with Son Clave.

Thus, as a conguero, what you need to know is where the 2-side and 3-side are, regardless of whether it's Son or Rumba Clave, and to know which side of your marcha (if it has 2 different sides) goes with which side of the clave.

The names of the different types of clave rhythms are also the source of frequent confusion. What we call "Son Clave" is this book is sometimes called "Puerto Rican Clave", and what we call "Rumba Clave" is sometimes called "Cuban Clave" or *"Clave de Guaguancó"*. We've heard the term *"Clave Cubana"* used for both types. The naming confusion even extends to the numbers. The rhythm we call "3-2 Rumba Clave":

...is sometimes called "2-3" by those who don't read music, because of the distance between the notes as opposed to their placement relative to the beats. For more on this often humorous debate, and more on clave in general, we refer you to the internet articles published at http:// clave.timba.com

"Playing the big drum on the 3-side"

This is another area where trying to be too rigid will get you into nothing but trouble! Let's look again at the way that Marcha 4 lines up with the clave:

Marcha 4	B	T	S	T	B	T	o	o	B	T	S	O	O	S	o	o
2-3 Rumba Clave			X		X				X		X					X

Tomás presents this marcha so that the low tones occur on the 3-side. This is often referred to as "playing the big drum on the 3-side" and in many Latin playing situations, it's considered very wrong to play this figure on the 2-side. However, take this with a grain of salt because when you get to the Timba marchas in Volume III you'll find many examples where these same two low drum tones occur on the 2-side.

"Clave Changes" and "Jumping the Clave"

As we pointed out above, the flow of the melody and harmony cause the listener to perceive the phrases of the music as beginning on the 2-side ("2-3 Clave") or the 3-side ("3-2 Clave"). A good arranger will write musical phrases which flow naturally with the clave, but what if one section sounds better starting on the 3-side and another on the 2-side? One solution is to devise a transitional phrase which is a half a clave longer or shorter than normal. For example:

Phrase 1: 2-3-2-3-2-3-2-3 etc
Transitional Phrase: 2-3-2
Phrase 2: 3-2-3-2-3-2-3-2 etc.

In this example, the alternating flow of the clave is uninterrupted but the perceived clave changes from 2-3 to 3-2. Of course, as we pointed out above, the perceived beginning of the phrase is the ear of the beholder, so the arranger's skill and creativity, or lack thereof, can intentionally or unintentionally result in varying percentages of listeners perceiving a clave change. A skillful arranger, if desired, can make the change so obvious that virtually all listeners perceive the clave change in the same place, but the same skillful arranger may prefer to leave the "plot" open to multiple interpretations. It's all a matter of artistic choice.

The arranger can also "jump the clave" by intentionally constructing the chart so that the percussionists are required to play the 2-side or the 3-side twice in a row. While easier for dancers, this is significantly harder for the musicians because everyone has to agree in advance, at rehearsal, to "jump the clave" at the same place. It's no longer a question of perception, but a matter of cold hard facts. You have to alter the natural flow of the clave and you have to do it at a prescribed moment in time.

For some reason, a particularly high percentage of the greatest masterpieces of all Latin music are heavily-laden with clave changes. Brilliant examples of the first type of clave change can be found in *"Todos vuelven"* by Rubén Blades, and *"Bamboleo"* by the Fania All-Stars. For equally brilliant examples of "jumping the clave", listen to *"No me mires a los ojos"* by Issac Delgado, *"Por encima del nivel"* by Los Van Van, or *"Extraños ateos"* by David Calzado y La Charanga Habanera.

The subject of clave changes is further explored at http://clave.timba.com. For further study of clave and Latin music in general, look for David Peñalosa's upcoming 7-volume series.

APPENDIX 2: Marchas in 8ths Notes

Marcha 1 – Marcha Cerrada – DVD Chapters 73 & 74

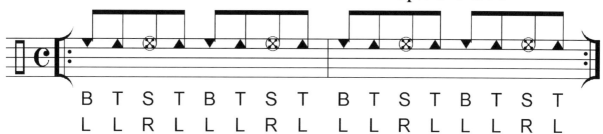

B T S T B T S T B T S T B T S T
L L R L L L R L L L R L L L R L

Marcha 2 – Tumbao (one drum) – DVD Chapters 75 & 76

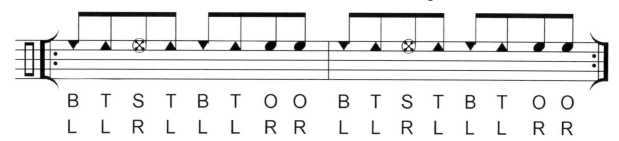

B T S T B T O O B T S T B T O O
L L R L L L R R L L R L L L R R

Marcha 3 – DVD Chapters 77 & 78

B T S B B T O O B T S B B T O O
L L R L R R L L R R L R L L R R

Marcha 4 – Tumbao (2 drums) – DVD Chapters 79 & 80

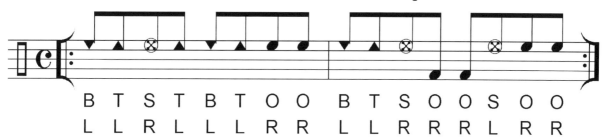

B T S B T O O B T S O O S O O
L L R L L L R R L L R R R L R R

Marcha 5 – Chachachá (one drum) – DVD Chapters 81 & 82

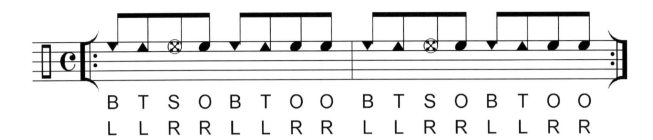

```
B T S O B T O O   B T S O B T O O
L L R R L L R R   L L R R L L R R
```

Marcha 6 – Chachachá (two drums) – DVD Chapters 84 & 85

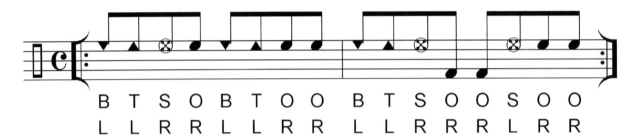

```
B T S O B T O O   B T S O O S O O
L L R R L L R R   L L R R R L R R
```

Marcha 7 – Bolero – DVD Chapters 85 & 86

```
B T S T B O O O   B T S T B O O O
L L R L L R L R   L L R L L R L R
```

APPENDIX 3: TOMÁS CRUZ: SELECTED DISCOGRAPHY

Paulito FG y su Élite
(Nueva Fania NF 104)

Tomasito's first commercial recording was made in 1996. The album has been re-issued with two different titles: "Paulito FG y su Élite" and "El bueno soy yo". It's an excellent Timba album, but we recommend starting your collection with Paulito's "Con la conciencia tranquila", released the following year, and then come back to this one.

"Gracias Formell"
Juan Ceruto
(Geminis Productions)

In 1997, arranger Juan Ceruto recorded this tribute album of modernized arrangements of classic compositions by Los Van Van's Juan Formell. The band is an all-star group comprised of the best Cuban singers and musicians of the era, with Tomás on congas and a guest appearance by another great Cuban conguero, Miguel "Angá" Díaz. The album was also released as **"Forbidden Cuba of the 90's: Gracias Formell" (RMM RMD 82249)** and more recently on the Ciocan Music label. It's an excellent introduction to about 20 of Timba's most important figures.

"Con la conciencia tranquila"
Paulito FG y su Élite
(Nueva Fania NF 108)

Many experts call "Con la conciencia" the greatest Cuban album of the 90's, and it was the fascination with this modern masterpiece that led the coauthors to seek out Tomás Cruz and persuade him to write this series of books. It's an excellent example of all the other concepts taught throughout this course and one of the principal subjects of Volume III of this series.

"El puente"
Manolín, El Médico de la Salsa
(Ciocan Music HMC2605)

Manolín was the most popular artist in Cuba in the second half of the 90's before running into trouble with the government and defecting to the United States. Tomasito joined the group when it reformed in Miami. "El puente" is a live double album recorded with Reinier Guerra playing drums and Tomás on congas. Tomás later over-dubbed the güiro parts in the studio. This historic live concert is a powerful example of Tomasito's playing and of the Timba genre which will be studied in depth in Volume III of this series.

Recording DVD Chapters
Santa Cruz, California
January, 2003
Photo by Tom Ehrlich

With Eduardo "Chaka" Nápoles
Miami, 2002 – Photo by Kevin Moore

With drummer Yoel Páez
Photo by Yoel Páez
71

35289555R00042

Made in the USA
San Bernardino, CA
21 June 2016